Sarbanes-Oxley for Nonprofit Boards

A New Governance Paradigm

PEGGY M. JACKSON, DPA, CPCU

WILEY

John Wiley & Sons, Inc.

For general information on our other products and services, or technical support, please contact our Customer Care Department within the United States at 800-762-2974, outside the United States at 317-572-3993, or fax 317-572-4002.

Wiley also publishes its books in a variety of electronic formats. Some content that appears in print may not be available in electronic books.

For more information about Wiley products, visit our Web site at http://www.wiley.com.

Library of Congress Cataloging-in-Publication Data:

Jackson, Peggy M.
    Sarbanes-Oxley for nonprofit boards : a new governance paradigm / Peggy M. Jackson.
        p. cm.
    Includes index.
    ISBN-13: 978-0-471-79037-2 (cloth)
    ISBN-10: 0-471-79037-0 (cloth)
        1. Nonprofit organizations—United States—Management.   2. United States. Sarbanes-Oxley Act of 2002.   3. Nonprofit organizations—Law and legislation—United States.   4. Nonprofit organizations—Accounting—Law and legislation—United States.   I. Title.
    HD62.6.J335 2006
    657'.980973—dc22

                                                        0000000000

Printed in the United States of America

10 9 8 7 6 5 4 3 2 1

This book is dedicated with love and gratitude to
the Reverend Elizabeth Carl and Ms. Victoria Hill

Contents

Acknowledgments

I would like to thank my editor, Susan McDermott, and the wonderful staff at John Wiley & Sons for their help and support in the writing of this book.

I would also like to acknowledge the support and encouragement that I receive from friends, family, and colleagues. Professor Al McLemore of California Maritime Academy provided much-needed resources in the completion of this manuscript. Paul, Rick, and Jan keep things in humorous perspective. I am also grateful for the support from my Business Alliance colleagues at the San Francisco Chamber of Commerce and from my colleagues in the San Francisco Junior League. You have been steadfast in cheering me on and a constant source of inspiration.

—PMJ

Preface

Membership on a nonprofit board should never be an "easy" assignment. It should be challenging work that results in a sense of satisfaction and a job well done—but never a walk in the park. The nonprofit world has changed dramatically in the past three years, and never more dramatically than in the new expectations of nonprofit boards. The bar has been raised to a higher level than ever before. Nonprofit boards have been told that they will be held accountable for *everything* that takes place in the nonprofit. The old cliché that management handles all of those things is no longer acceptable to regulators and legislators.

The book is intended to help nonprofit boards and their leadership understand what is expected of them and their nonprofits in this new environment, and how to implement Sarbanes-Oxley requirements and best practices. *The areas covered in this legislation really are practices that should have been in place all along.* The enhanced expectations of Sarbanes-Oxley apply to all organizations, publicly traded companies, private firms, and nonprofits. Boards need to reclaim their role as the ultimate authority in the nonprofit and actively supervise their only employee, the executive director. Board members and leaders alike need to acknowledge their legal and ethical obligations and take action. Boards need to revisit their governance and oversight responsibilities because they will now be held accountable by federal and state authorities for the management and operation of the nonprofit.

Being a member of a highly functional board can be an exhilarating experience. Sarbanes-Oxley compliance and best practices can boost your board's quality and productivity.

About the Author

Peggy M. Jackson, DPA, CPCU, is a consultant and nationally recognized lecturer in risk management, business continuity planning and Sarbanes-Oxley compliance. She is a principal with Adjunct LLC and a founding partner of the Fogarty, Jackson & Associates Consulting Group in San Francisco, California. Dr. Jackson has coauthored several books published by Wiley including *Managing Risk in Nonprofit Organizations, Sarbanes-Oxley for Nonprofits, Sarbanes-Oxley and Nonprofit Management: Skills, Techniques, and Methods* and *Sarbanes-Oxley for Nonprofit Boards*. She divides her time and consulting practice between her homes in the San Francisco Bay Area and the Washington, DC metro area.

CHAPTER 1

History and Legislative Background of the Sarbanes-Oxley Act of 2002 and State Nonprofit Accountability Legislation

On August 12, 2002, Senator Charles Grassley (R–Iowa) sent an angry letter to Marsha Johnson Evans, newly installed president of the American Red Cross, demanding an explanation for what was apparently false information contained in a response to an inquiry from his office about the Red Cross handling of the Liberty Fund monies that were collected to support September 11 victims' families. Subsequent to the Red Cross's initial response, Senator Grassley had received information that directly contradicted the Red Cross's assertions. [See Appendix A]

His letter to Ms. Evans continues:

> Further, I was surprised by findings relating to a "surprise" audit of 27 Red Cross chapters that KPMG performed on September 18, 2001. In a memorandum to Dr. Healy and other high-ranking Red Cross officials including its Chief Financial Operator, Jack Campbell, KPMG identified problems at the chapters relating to how they processed and allocated donations received

since 9/11. KPMG's findings range from chapters mishandling "9/11" donations by keeping the money instead of transmitting the funds to the Liberty Disaster Relief Fund (Liberty Fund), to failing to follow national accounting procedures. For example:

- Alexandria, Virginia, "Chapter has not counted lockbox donations since 9/11, but assumes that most will be coded as local funds."
- Bergen Crossroads, NJ, "Due to this chapter's location, almost all funds were designated [World Trade Center]. For non-designated funds, coded as local."
- Los Angeles, California, "Chapter has no accurate accounting for funds received after 9/11, at least $500,000 in total."
- Montgomery County, MD, "Amount collected prior to 9/11 unknown due to backlog in accounting reconciliations (recent transition in accounting department)."
- Pine Tree, ME, "Cash/checks unlocked at all times."
- Savannah, GA, "Chapter could not provide information regarding cash/checks collected."

Taken as a whole, these documents reveal a history of serious financial mismanagement by Red Cross chapters that I find troubling. However, I am more concerned that Red Cross senior management appears to take an attitude that bad news from local chapters is all best swept under the rug. The Red Cross' indifference to these major accountability problems was verbalized by Mr. Campbell during a CBS Evening News interview broadcast on July 30, 2002:

CBS News Correspondent Sharyl Attkisson: "Weren't you troubled by the results of the audits?"

Campbell: "Actually, we were not troubled by the results of the audits at all. There was no recognition of any kind of problem."

As surprising as this denial may be, it is consistent with other high-profile scandals in the private sector. Enron, WorldCom, and other corporate scandals may have led to the passage of Sarbanes-Oxley legislation, but clearly the private sector does not have the corner on duplicity. Nonprofit organizations including the American Red Cross, United Way of the National Capital Area, James Beard, and Boy Scouts of America have had very public scandals and have come under scrutiny by lawmakers at the federal and state levels.

WHAT IS THE SARBANES-OXLEY LEGISLATION ABOUT?

The Public Company Accounting Reform and Investor Protection Act was passed in 2002 in the wake of the Enron corporate scandal. The act is commonly referred to as the Sarbanes-Oxley Act (SOX), named after Senator Paul Sarbanes (D-MD) and Representative Michael Oxley (R-OH), who were its main sponsors. Although SOX was initially intended to raise the bar for integrity and competence for publicly traded companies—companies that have stockholders—its effect has been to promote greater accountability within both the nonprofit and the private sector.

The Sarbanes-Oxley Act is the latest in a long progression of regulatory reform aimed at rectifying corporate misdeeds. SOX has its roots in the Great Depression, which began in 1929 and lasted more than a decade, and was one of the deepest economic slumps to ever affect the United States, Europe, and other industrialized countries. Although the actual causes are still intensely debated, some factors believed to have contributed to the Great Depression in the United States were the mass stock speculation that occurred during the 1920s; a general imbalance of purchasing power and wealth in that a large percentage of the population was poor while a small percentage was very wealthy; the laissez-faire economic philosophy adhered to by Presidents Warren Harding (1920–1923), Calvin Coolidge (1923–1928), and Herbert Hoover (1929–1933); and the catastrophic crash of stock prices on the New York Stock Exchange (NYSE) in 1929. On October 29, 1929, known as Black Tuesday, the U.S. stock market crashed, and the value of stock steeply plummeted. Black Tuesday was one of the worst trading days in the history of the stock market. Stock prices collapsed and most of the financial gains of the previous year were wiped out within the first few hours of the market's opening. Since most Americans viewed the stock market as the chief indicator of the health of the economy, the 1929 crash destroyed public confidence in both the stock market and in the U.S. economy.

Stock value continued to fall for approximately three years, until late 1932. By that time, stocks had lost 80 percent of their value from 1929. Individual investors suffered devastating losses; overnight, large fortunes simply melted away. Many banks and other financial institutions, particularly those holding a large portion of stocks in their portfolios, also suffered severe losses in assets. By 1933, 11,000 of the 25,000 banks in the nation had failed. In part, the 1929 crash was blamed on wildly inflated stock prices, poor monetary policies imposed by the Federal Reserve Board, fraud, concealed or misleading financial information, the rampant of buying of stock on margin, and inadequate controls on trading in the U.S. market. In 1932, the newly elected president, Franklin D. Roosevelt, and Congress sought to regulate the market by imposing controls on trading and requiring organizations that were offering securities for public sale to provide financial and other significant information about those securities.

Two important pieces of legislation emerged from this turbulent time. The Securities Act of 1933, which is frequently referred to as the truth in securities law, focused on assuring that investors are fully informed about the financial aspects of securities being offered for sale and on prohibiting deceit, misrepresentation, and other fraud in securities transactions. The Securities Exchange Act of 1934 created the Securities and Exchange Commission (SEC) and gave it the power to regulate many aspects of the securities industry. The act also provided the SEC with the authority to require periodic reporting of financial information by organizations that offered publicly traded securities and gave the SEC the power to register, regulate, and oversee brokerage firms, transfer agents, and the stock exchanges. Some of the important powers these two acts gave the SEC include:

- Regulate and register stock exchanges as well as all securities listed on an exchange.
- Regulate investment advisers and all dealers and brokers who are members of an organized exchange.
- Require that audited and current financial reports be filed.
- Set accounting standards.
- Prohibit all forms of stock price manipulation, such as insider trading.

The availability of properly audited and current financial reports enables investors to make informed and rational choices about whether to invest in a particular company. The audited financial reports are available from the organizations selling the securities in their stockholders' annual reports. The SEC continues to protect investors today, adding stability to investors' confidence and the markets in general. Additional controls on the market after the 1987 crash regarding program trading and the institution of market shutdown mechanisms called circuit breakers helped to smooth out some of the volatility in the market.

Twenty-First-Century Corporate and Accounting Scandals

At the beginning of the twenty-first century, the U.S. market and its investors were stunned by a string of corporate and accounting scandals. For several years, the Enron Corporation, an energy company, participated in a number of partnership transactions that lost the organization a substantial amount of money. In 2001, Enron reported that it had failed to follow generally accepted accounting practices in its financial statements for 1997 through 2001 by excluding these unprofitable transactions. In these erroneous financial statements, the organization reported large profits when, in fact, it had lost a total of $586 million during those years. Neither internal nor external controls detected the financial losses disguised as profits. The revelation of the erroneous financial reporting led to a collapse in the price of Enron stock, which fell from $83 per share in December 2000 to less than $1 per share in December 2001. However, some of Enron's managers made millions of dollars by selling their company stock before its price plummeted. Other investors, including Enron employees who had invested a large portion of their retirement portfolios in Enron stock, experienced substantial losses.

Role of Arthur Andersen LLP   The CPA firm of Arthur Andersen LLP, which had been one of the largest accounting firms in the world, served as Enron's auditor throughout the years of erroneous statements. The firm allegedly "overlooked" Enron's questionable accounting practices because it was making a large amount of money providing Enron with consulting services and did not want to lose the consulting business. The firm was indicted by the U.S. Department of Justice, and in 2002, Arthur Andersen LLP was convicted of obstructing justice by shredding Enron–related documents requested by the SEC. Andersen's role in the Enron scandal is reflected in the SOX requirements to ensure auditor independence.

WorldCom   In 2002, WorldCom, Inc., a prominent telecommunications company, admitted that it had failed to report more than $7 billion in expenses over five quarterly periods. Its financial statements indicated that

WorldCom had been profitable over those quarters, when the company had actually lost $1.2 billion. WorldCom's market worth plunged from $200 billion to only $10 billion in July. In July 2002, WorldCom filed for Chapter 11 bankruptcy, causing concerns among its investors, creditors, and telecommunication customers.

Enron and WorldCom were not the only companies that had questionable financial statements. Other corporate and accounting scandals included Tyco, Adelphia Communications, Xerox, and Global Crossing. These scandals understandably shook the public's confidence in the capital markets and in the integrity of corporate financial statements. In response to the lack of public confidence and the downward plummet in the stock market, the 107th Congress passed the Public Company Accounting Reform and Investor Protection Act, which was signed into law by President George W. Bush on July 30, 2002.

Importance of Sarbanes-Oxley Legislation

Many would agree that the SOX is the single most important piece of legislation affecting corporate governance, financial disclosure, and public accounting since the passage of the Securities Act of 1933 and the Securities Exchange Act of 1934. SOX contains sweeping reforms for issuers of publicly traded securities, auditors, corporate board members, and lawyers. It adopts new provisions intended to deter and punish corporate and accounting fraud and corruption, and provides stiff penalties for noncompliance. In essence, SOX seeks to protect the interest of shareholders and employees by improving the overall quality of financial reporting, independent audits, corporate accountability, and accounting services for public companies. As can be seen in Exhibit 1.1, SOX consists of 11 titles, with each title having multiple sections.

Several sections of the law address requirements and/or best practices for nonprofits and for private companies.

Title II

Title II of SOX details the rules to establish independence of the auditor from the company being audited. It defines which additional services the auditing firm may and may not provide, defines and prohibits conflicts of interest between auditors and the audited company, requires that the audited firm rotates its auditors on a regular basis, and requires the auditing committee of the audited company to be responsible for the oversight of its auditors.

Titles III and IV

Titles III and IV of SOX detail the responsibilities and roles to be played the audited company in regard to the audit and reports. For example, the principal executive and financial officers of the company are directly responsible to certify that the information in the annual or quarterly reports required by the SEC Act of 1934 is accurate, complete, and fairly presented. In addition, there are rules regarding insider trading and the professional responsibility for attorneys to report violations of securities law or breach of fiduciary duty. The titles also outline the disclosure requirements of relevant financial information, such as off-balance-sheet arrangements and relationships.

Titles VIII, IX, X, and XI

Titles VIII, IX, X, and XI outline the penalties for securities fraud and document destruction or alteration; create whistleblower protection for employee informants; and establish corporate responsibility for financial reports. Title IX provides that each periodic report containing financial statements filed with the SEC must be accompanied by a written statement by the issuer's chief executive officer and chief financial officer certifying that the report fully complies with the 1934 act and that information contained in the periodic report "fairly presents, in all material respects, the financial condition and results of operations of the issuer."

Relevance of SOX to Nonprofits

Currently, only a few of the provisions in SOX directly apply to nonprofit organizations. Nonprofits are required to adhere to provisions that provide protection to employees who report suspected fraud or other illegal activities and to provisions that address the destruction or falsification of records or documents.

The nonprofit sector has experienced its own recent scandals of perceived wrongdoing and fiscal mismanagement. For example, the United Way and the American Red Cross have received substantial unfavorable

EXHIBIT 1.1   SOX LISTING OF TITLES
AND SECTIONS

Title	Section
I. Public Company Accounting Oversight Board	101: Establishment, administrative provision 102: Registration with the Board 103: Auditing, quality control, and independence standards and rules 104: Inspections of registered public accounting firms 105: Investigations and disciplinary proceedings 106: Foreign public accounting firms 107: Commission oversight of the Board 108: Accounting standards 109: Funding
II. Auditor Independence **Best Practices for nonprofits come from this section.**	201: Services outside the scope of practice of auditors 202: Preapproval requirements 203: Audit partner rotation 204: Auditor reports to audit committees 205: Conforming amendments 206: Conflicts of interest 207: Study of mandatory rotation of registered public accounting firms 208: Commission authority 209: Considerations by appropriate state regulatory authorities
III. Corporate Responsibility **Best Practices for nonprofits come from this section.**	301: Public company audit committees 302: Corporate responsibility for financial reports 303: Improper influence on conduct of audits 304: Forfeiture of certain bonuses and profits 305: Officer and director bars and penalties 306: Insider trades during pension fund blackout periods 307: Rules of professional responsibility for attorneys 308: Fair funds for investors
IV. Enhanced Financial Disclosures **Best Practices for nonprofits come from this section.**	401: Disclosures in periodic reports 402: Enhanced conflict-of-interest provisions 403: Disclosure of transactions involving management and principal stockholders 404: Management assessment of internal controls

Title	Section
	405: Exemption
	406: Code of ethics for senior financial officers
	407: Disclosure of audit committee financial expert
	408: Enhanced review of periodic disclosures by issuers
	409: Real-time issuer disclosures
VIII. Corporate and Criminal Fraud Accountability Document preservation Whistleblower protection **Best Practices for nonprofits come from this section. Sections 802 and 806 (document preservation and whistleblower protection) are legal requirements for *all* organizations, including nonprofits.**	801: Short title 802: Criminal penalties for altering documents 803: Debts nondischareable if incurred in violation of securities fraud laws 804: Statute of limitations for securities fraud 805: Review of federal sentencing guidelines for obstruction of justice and extensive criminal fraud 806: Protection for employees of publicly traded companies who provide evidence of fraud 807: Criminal penalties for defrauding shareholders of publicly traded companies
IX. White-Collar Crime Penalty **Best Practices for nonprofits come from this section.**	901: Short title 902: Attempts and conspiracies to commit criminal fraud offenses 903: Criminal penalties for mail and wire fraud 904: Criminal penalties for violations of the Employee Retirement Income Security Act of 1974 905: Amendment to sentencing guidelines relating to certain white-collar offenses 906: Corporate responsibility for financial reports
XI. Corporate Fraud and Accountability **Best Practices for nonprofits come from this section. Section 1107 (retaliation against informants) is a legal requirement for all organizations, including nonprofits.**	1101: Short title 1102: Tampering with a record or otherwise impeding an official proceeding 1103: Temporary freeze authority for the Securities and Exchange Commission 1104: Amendment to the Federal Sentencing Guidelines 1105: Authority of the Commission to prohibit persons from serving as officers or directors 1106: Increased criminal penalties under Securities Exchange Act of 1934 1107: Retaliation against informants

media coverage of their apparent failures in accountability and adherence to mission. Incidents such as these have cast the nonprofit sector in an unfavorable light and have damaged the public's trust in the integrity and the public benefit of nonprofits. Although the majority of the SOX provisions currently apply only to publicly traded corporations and not to nonprofit organizations, nonprofits could benefit operationally from adopting some of the SOX rules as best practices. In addition, voluntarily adhering to the SOX gold standards would create greater credibility and ability to recruit high-quality board members as well as attract the favorable attention of major donors, foundations, and other funding sources.

If the nonprofit sector wishes to retain its current level of relative self-regulation, nonprofit leaders need to make a visible effort to improve organizational governance and accountability. If this does not occur, nonprofits may come under additional unwanted government regulation. Some state attorneys general have already suggested that additional provisions of SOX should be applied to nonprofits. In order to avoid the imposition of external regulation, the nonprofit sector needs to show the government and the public that it can regulate nonprofit governance effectively.

CURRENT LEGISLATIVE ENVIRONMENT FOR NONPROFITS

U.S. Senate Finance Committee Hearings on Nonprofit Accountability, June 2004

Although the features of the Sarbanes-Oxley legislation may on the surface appear to have more impact on the private sector, the public sector (i.e. government) push for greater accountability includes the independent sector (i.e., the nonprofit world) as well. This section discusses the United States Senate Finance Committee June 22, 2004, hearings on Charitable Giving Problems and Best Practices, along with the highlights of recent California "Sarbanes-Oxley clone" legislation (SB1262) signed into law on September 29, 2004. The common theme of the testimony of witnesses, the congressional staff papers, and the California "Nonprofit Integrity Act" (SB1262) is that nonprofit organizations have, through fiscal and governance abuses, diminished public trust. Public outrage fueled these congressional hearings on nonprofit abuses.

Senate Finance Committee: Grassley "White Paper"   Subsequent to the hearings and testimony, a staff discussion paper was released with recommendations for closer regulation of nonprofits. At the present time, these are simply a series of recommendations by congressional staff, but the tone and reach of the recommendations should be taken seriously by every nonprofit regardless of size.

The preface to the document instructs the reader that:

> The document reflects proposals for reforms and best practices in the area of tax-exempt organizations based on staff investigations and research as well as proposals from practitioners, officers and directors of charities, academia and other interested parties. This document is a work-in-progress and is meant to encourage and foster additional comments and suggestions as the Finance Committee continues to consider possible legislation.[1]

Some of the proposals in this document include:

Five-year review of tax-exempt status by the IRS.   The White Paper recommends that:

> On every fifth anniversary of the IRS's determination of the tax-exempt status of an organization that is required to apply for such status, the organization would be required to file with the IRS such information as would enable the IRS to determine whether the organization continues to be organized and operated exclusively for an exempt purposes (i.e., whether the original determination letter should remain in effect). Information to be filed would include current articles of incorporation and by-laws, conflicts of interest policies, evidence of accreditation, management policies regarding best practices, a detailed narrative about the organization's practices, and financial statements.

What would this mean for nonprofits? This recommendation would require nonprofits to submit documentation every five years that proves to the Internal Revenue Service that the organization continues to be in compliance with its 501(c)(3) designation. The following list of documents is particularly enlightening about the intent of this proposal.

- *Current articles of incorporation and by-laws.* The nonprofit would need to be clear about how its operations and governance continue to be in harmony with its founding documents

- *Conflict-of-interest policies.* The nonprofit would have to provide evidence of a conflict-of-interest policy and, most likely, proof that board members and senior management have completed annual affidavits identifying real or potential conflicts of interest.

- *Evidence of accreditation.* This document would be based on another recommendation, which is that nonprofits be required to obtain specific accreditation. (This recommendation is discussed later in this section.)

- *Management policies regarding best practices.* The nonprofit would be required to develop and submit written policies that demonstrate that the organization is implementing best practices in management and governance.

- *A detailed narrative about the organization's practices.* This document would require the nonprofit to provide a detailed explanation about what the organization does and why it is necessary/desirable in the community.

- *Financial statements.* These statements would be supplemental to the Form 990 that is required on an annual basis.

Form 990s—Proposals for Reform   The White Paper recommends that nonprofits improve quality and scope of Form 990 and financial statements:

> In a report to the Finance Committee, the General Accounting Office found significant problems in the accuracy and completeness of Form 990. Other studies, including by the General Accounting Office, have highlighted that there are no common standards for filing the Form 990, and thus similarly situated charities can have very different Form 990s. Because of the significant role played by the Form 990 in public and governmental oversight of tax-exempt organizations, some reforms are necessary to ensure accurate, complete, timely, consistent, and informative reporting by exempt organizations.

What does this mean for nonprofits? The Internal Revenue Service recognizes that there are no common standards for completion of Form 990s. The reform proposal seeks to identify reforms that will introduce a standardized way to submit Form 990s.

Form 990s would require signature by chief executive officer.

> Require that the chief executive officer (or equivalent officer) of a tax-exempt organization sign a declaration under penalties of perjury that the chief executive officer has put in place processes and procedures to ensure that the organization's Federal information return and tax return (including Form 990T) complies with the Internal Revenue Code and that the CEO was provided reasonable assurance of the accuracy and completeness of all material aspects of the return. This declaration would be part of the information for tax returns.

What does this mean for nonprofits? This proposal would require a nonprofit CEO to sign an affidavit that "under penalties of perjury . . ." the organization's Form 990 complies with the Internal Revenue Code and the CEO is providing assurance of the accuracy and completeness of all material aspects of the return. (The financials accurately reflect the financial position of the nonprofit.) This affidavit would be part of the information or tax return.

Based on recent events in the nonprofit world, if this proposal was law, some very high-profile nonprofit executives would be going to jail. The recommendation here is clearly that nonprofit executives and board members should be held to the same criminal liability standards as those of their private sector counterparts.

Penalties for failure to file complete and accurate form 990.

> The present law penalty for failure to file or to include required information is $20/day up to the lesser of $10,000 or 5 percent of gross receipts per return (increased to $100/day up to $50,000 per return for organizations with gross receipts over $1 million in a year). Under the proposal, the penalty for failure to file would be doubled and for organizations with gross receipts over $2 million per year, the present law penalty would be tripled. Failure to file a required 990 for two consecutive years (or for three of four years) could result in loss of tax exemption, or other penalties such as loss of status as an organization to which deductible contributions may be made.

What does this mean for nonprofits? There will be severe penalties for failing to file a Form 990. The proposals recommend loss of tax exemption, or loss of status as an organization to which deductible contributions may be made. For a nonprofit, this means the organization can no longer tell donors that their contributions are tax-exempt. In other words, the "non-profit" is out of business.

Required disclosure of performance goals, activities, and expenses in Form 990 and in financial statements.   Charitable organizations with over $250,000 in gross receipts would be required to include in the Form 990 a detailed description of the organization's annual performance goals and measurements for meeting those goals (to be established by the board of directors) for the past year and goals for the coming year. The purpose of this requirement would be to assist donors to better determine an organization's accomplishments and goals in deciding whether to donate, and not as a point of review by the IRS. Charitable organizations would be required to disclose material changes in activities, operations, or structure. Charitable organizations would be required to accurately report the charity's expenses, including any joint cost allocations, in their financial statements and Form 990s. Exempt organizations would be required to report how often the board of directors met and how often the board met, without the CEO (or equivalent) present.

What does this mean for nonprofits? Transparency is the predominant theme of these recommendations. The congressional staff may have been spurred on by the volume of public complaints about nonprofit organizations that, for every donor dollar, contribute very little to programs. In recent years, the media has conducted many investigations of bogus charities, and certainly some charities that are household names have also abused donor trust by misdirecting donations to exorbitant salaries, expenses, and other abuses. Note that these disclosures are required to be presented on Form 990. The accuracy of these disclosures could carry criminal liability if the other proposal on CEO signatures is enacted into law.

Nonprofits Would Be Required to Make Certain Documents Publicly Available   Public oversight is critical to ensuring that an exempt organization continues to operate in accordance with its tax-exempt status. For charitable organizations, public oversight provides donors with vital information for determining which organizations have the programs and practices that will ensure that contributions will be spent as intended. Oversight is facilitated under present law by mandated public disclosure of information returns and applications for tax-exempt status, but more can be done.

Disclosure of financial statements.

Exempt organizations would be required to disclose to the public the organization's financial statements.

Web site disclosure.

Exempt organizations with a Web site would be required to post on such site any return that is required to be made public by present law, the organization's application for tax exemption, the organization's determination letter from the IRS, and the organization's financial statements for the five most recent years.

What does this mean for nonprofits? Although the text recognizes that there are current public oversight opportunities, the authors comment that the nonprofit world could be doing more to provide transparency. The recommendations are, again, aimed at ensuring that the public has access to information that would be vital to their making a decision to make a donation. Of particular note is the recommendation that the nonprofit's Web site be employed to present not only those documents currently required (Form 990) but also the organization's:

- Application for tax exemption
- Determination letter from the IRS
- Financial statements from the five most recent years

Proposals Regarding Nonprofit Boards

The White Paper makes these recommendations:

Board duties. The duties of a board that are described in this document would also be the duties of a trustee for a charitable trust. A charitable organization shall be managed by its board of directors or trustees (in the case of a charitable trust). In performing duties, a board member has to perform his or her duties in good faith; with the care an ordinarily prudent person in a like position would exercise under similar circumstances; and in a manner the director reasonably believes to be in the best interests of the mission, goals, and purposes of the corporation. An individual who has special skills or expertise has a duty to use such skills or expertise. Federal liability for breach of these duties would be established. Any compensation consultant to the charity must be hired by and report to the board, and must be independent. Compensation for all management positions must be approved annually and in advance unless there is no change in compensation other than an inflation adjustment. Compensation arrangements must be explained and justified and publicly disclosed (with such explanation) in a manner that can be understood by an individual with a basic business background.

The board must establish basic organizational and management policies and procedures of organization and review any proposed deviations. The board must establish, review, and approve program objectives and performance measures and, review and approve significant transactions. The board must review and approve the auditing and accounting principles and practices used in preparing the organization's financial statements and must retain and replace the organization's independent auditor. An independent auditor must be hired by the board, and each such auditor may be retained only five years. The board must review and approve the organization's budget and financial objectives as well as significant investments, joint ventures, and business transactions. The board must oversee the conduct of the corporation's business and evaluate whether the business is being properly managed.

The board must establish a conflict-of-interest policy (which would be required to be disclosed with Form 990) and require a summary of conflicts determinations made during the 990 reporting year. The board must establish and oversee a compliance program to address regulatory and liability concerns.

The board must establish procedures to address complaints and prevent retaliation against whistleblowers. All of these requirements must be confirmed on Form 990. Relaxation of certain of these rules might be appropriate for smaller tax-exempt organizations.

Board composition. The board shall be comprised of no less than 3 members and no greater than 15.

What does this mean for the nonprofits? The proposals for reform indicate that the traditional legal standards of care, loyalty, and obedience could be incorporated into a law governing board member behavior. The proposal clearly indicates that the board is regarded as the final authority in the management of the nonprofit organization and, as such, will be held accountable for the implementation of such policies as a conflict-of-interest policy and whistleblower protection. Board size appears to be capped at 15, but the authors did not present clear reasons for this limitation.

The entire board could now be held directly accountable for the executive director's compensation package. Many nonprofit boards do not have access to the compensation package of the executive director, as this has come under the exclusive purview of the board's executive committee.

Proposals for Government Encouragement of Best Practices

Accreditation. The White Paper recommends:

> There would be an authorization of $10 million to the IRS to support accreditation of charities nationwide, in states, as well as accreditation of charities of particular classes (e.g., private foundations, land conservation groups, etc.). The IRS would have the authority to contract with tax-exempt organizations that would create and manage an accreditation program to establish best practices and give accreditation to members that meet best practices and review organizations on an ongoing basis for compliance. The IRS would have the authority to base charitable status or authority of a charity to accept charitable donations on whether an organization is accredited.

What does this mean for nonprofits? This proposal seeks to empower the Internal Revenue Service with the authority to require accreditation of nonprofits as a requisite to accepting charitable donations. The authors are seeking to empower the IRS to add another layer of compliance to the Form 990 proposals and five-year reauthorization of nonprofits.

Oversight provisions. The White Paper recommends that:

> The Federal Government establish an Exempt Organization Hotline for reporting abuses by charities and complaints by donors and beneficiaries. Information sharing with State Attorneys General, the Federal Trade Commission, and the U.S. Postal Service for enforcement purposes, including referrals by the IRS and an annual report to Congress by the General Accounting Office of the results of such referrals.

This proposal would establish a hotline for anyone anywhere to file complaints about nonprofits and/or report abuses. Whether this is an anonymous hotline remains to be seen, but the authors appear to want to collect this information at a national level. How the complaints and claims would be investigated and by what agency also remains to be seen.

California's Nonprofit Integrity Act

Provisions That Apply to Nonprofits with Revenues in Excess of $2 Million

The state of California passed a Nonprofit Integrity Act (SB1282), which imposes many of the features of Sarbanes-Oxley legislation on nonprofits with revenues in excess of $2 million operating in that state.

Some of the key provisions of this law include:

- Nonprofits will be required to have an annual audit performed by a CPA who is "independent" as defined by U.S. Government auditing standards. The results of the audit will need to be made available to the public and the attorney general.

- Nonprofits will be required to have an audit committee whose membership cannot include staff and must not overlap more than 50 percent with the finance committee; the audit committee can include members who are not on the organization's board of directors.

What does this mean for nonprofits in California? To ensure greater accountability in executive compensation the law requires that the board approve the compensation, including benefits, of the corporation's president or CEO and its treasurer or CFO for the purposes of assuring that these executives' compensation package is reasonable.

What does this mean for nonprofits in California? Requires disclosure of written contracts between commercial fundraisers and nonprofits and available for review on demand from the attorney general's office. Fundraisers must be registered with the attorney general's office.

These points in the law apply to all nonprofits, regardless of revenue size, in California.

- Nonprofits must make their audits available to the public on the same basis as their IRS Form 990 if they prepare financial statements that are audited by a CPA.

- Except for emergencies, notice of a solicitation campaign by a "commercial fundraiser for charitable purposes" must be filed at least 10 days before the commencement of the solicitation campaign, events, or other services. Each contract must be signed by an official of the nonprofit, and include the contract provisions specified in the law.

• Regarding fundraising activities, the law states that a nonprofit must not misrepresent or mislead anyone about its purpose, or the nature, purpose, or beneficiary of a solicitation. Further, the law specifies that there be specific disclosures in any solicitation that the funds raised will be used for the charitable purpose as expressed in articles of incorporation or other governing documents. The nonprofit is expected to ensure that fundraising activities are adequately supervised to ensure that contracts and agreements are in order and that fundraising is conducted without intimidation or undue influence.

What does this mean for nonprofits in California? Nonprofits in California, regardless of their size, need to review their fundraising practices, particularly if some or all of their fundraising is outsourced to commercial fundraising firms. Nonprofits will be liable for abuses by vendors of fundraising services. As a practical matter, boards should insist that due diligence activities be conducted before contracting with any vendor, particularly those providing fundraising services. The California law, however, places strict parameters around third-party fundraising.

SUMMARY

Corporate and nonprofit malfeasance is, sadly, not a new development. The Sarbanes-Oxley Act and California's Nonprofit Integrity Act are intended to obligate nonprofit boards and senior management to conduct the business of the nonprofit in a more transparent and accountable fashion.

Whistleblower protection and document preservation policies are the two requirements for nonprofits from the Sarbanes-Oxley legislation. The legislation, however, puts forward a series of best practices that are rapidly becoming instituted as the new platinum standard in nonprofit management.

ENDNOTE

1. Senate Finance Committee White Paper, 2004, p. 1.

CHAPTER 2

Moving Nonprofit Governance into the Twenty-First Century

The [U.S. Senate] Finance Committee has been engaged in a bipartisan review of charities and reform of charities and it appears that the AU [American University] board could be a poster child for why review and reform are necessary.

Senator Charles Grassley (R-Iowa)[1]

Senator Grassley wrote these chilling words in an October 27, 2005, letter to Thomas Gottschalk, acting chair of the board of American University. The university had been rocked for months by a scandal involving financial mismanagement by its former president, Benjamin Ladner. Ladner has been accused of excessive spending for expenses related to travel and other perks. A subsequent audit found that Ladner had improperly charged $125,000 in personal and travel expenses to the university and that $398,000 in other charges are taxable income. Senator Grassley's letter goes on to allege that Ladner is also accused of failing to pay taxes on $400,000 of income for the last three years. The board approved a $3.75 million severance package for Ladner based on "the risks, costs and delay inherent in litigation."[2]

The overarching theme of Senator Grassley's letter to Gottschalk is the betrayal of public trust that resulted from the AU board's actions.

The Internal Revenue Code ("IRC") provides charities very special treatment. Most important is the exemption from income tax and the ability to receive tax-deductible contributions. It is therefore particularly troubling when an organization receives preferential tax treatment and then believes that it is proper to provide approximately $3.75 million in payments to an individual who has reportedly failed to pay taxes on nearly $400,000 in income (for the last three years) after the board terminated his employment. Such actions raise significant questions about what other things a charity that has such a cavalier attitude toward the tax laws might be doing, especially in light of escalating tuition increases.[3]

The Senate Finance Committee led the charge in investigating abuses within the nonprofit sector. As was illustrated in the excerpts from the White Paper in Chapter 1, it has launched a proposal to bring nonprofit management standards into line with generally accepted management practices

How Sarbanes-Oxley Legislation Has Changed Governance Expectations in All Economic Sectors

The Sarbanes-Oxley legislation prompted higher scrutiny of boards in the private and nonprofit world. In January 2005, New York Attorney General Eliot Spitzer forced board members of WorldCom to pay fines out of their private resources rather than simply allow the company's directors and officers (D&O) insurance policy to pay the claim.[4]

Senator Grassley and the Senate Finance Committee are focusing on nonprofits, with particular emphasis on their boards, because the source of the high-profile nonprofit scandals has been primarily board negligence or inattention. In Senator Grassley's letter to the AU board, he directed that they respond to four pages of questions addressing the board's decision making on Ladner's compensation, Internal Revenue Service filings, overall policies on executive compensation, and board governance and transparency. In his October 27, 2005, letter to Gottschalk, the senator raises these questions in terms of the American University's board governance and transparency:

- Discuss whether you believe that there is sufficient transparency regarding your highly compensated offers, directors, trustees and employees.

- Provide descriptions of all transactions with *disqualified* persons [meaning individuals who would not be permitted to bid on contracts such as board members] . . . Please provide copies of legal opinions and minutes from board meetings discussing these transaction . . . [for] the last three years for compensation, loans, property purchases/leases and services for over $100,000.
- Given the extraordinary troubling findings from the audit of the most recent time period [three years], please inform me of your plans to conduct a complete audit of the entire 11 years [of Ladner's employment].
- Provide your articles of incorporation, bylaws (in effect for the past 11 years), application for exempt status and IRS determination letter. For the past 11 years, please provide a brief description of individuals who served on the boards, a short biography, qualifications, how the board member was selected and how the board members serve the interests of the community.

These questions focus on board accountability, board member selection, due diligence (or the lack thereof), and how the board's actions correspond to the university's articles of incorporation and by-laws. The tone and content of the letter are unmistakable in emphasizing that Senator Grassley and the Finance Committee believe that the AU board is fully accountable for the scandal.

Donor Activism and Legislative Scrutiny

Stakeholders of corporations and nonprofits, whether they are shareholders or donors, do not want to be deceived about the use/return of money that is either invested or donated. The age of shareholder/donor activism has been ushered in via scandals such as Enron, United Way of the National Capital Area, the American Red Cross's Liberty Fund, WorldCom, Tyco, and other organizations, private sector and nonprofit alike. The public's patience with corporate deception is at an all-time low. Congress and state legislatures are feeling the pressure from their constituents to do something to restore public trust in these institutions.

Because the business models of nonprofits and private-sector firms are becoming ever more parallel, the "mom-and-pop" nonprofit is no longer a viable model in terms of donor confidence. Professionalism is the order of the day—as it should be. Donors expect that nonprofits will be good stewards of their donations, and in today's business climate, this means that nonprofits will be subject to the same scrutiny and regulatory applications as their private-sector counterparts.

The potential for keeping scandals in-house is rapidly dissipating. In today's media-driven environment, news outlets report on crises almost the minute these events are known. News crews from CNN and elsewhere are capable of covering a story within minutes of its occurrence. The scope of nonprofit scandals has grown significantly. In most of the nonprofit scandals that have been aggressively covered by the media in the past five years, the missing or misappropriated funds have totaled millions of dollars.

Role of the Enhanced IRS Enforcement in Raising Nonprofit Accountability Standards

The testimony of Mark Everson, IRS commissioner, at the Finance Committee's hearings in 2004 and 2005 introduced some important themes that provide critical clues for all nonprofit boards.

Increase in Size and Complexity of the Tax-Exempt Sector   The commissioner reported that this sector has grown:

> . . . the number of exempt entities on our master-file has increased by almost 500,000 since 1995, to 1.8 million today. In the period from FY 1998 to FY 2002 alone, the reported value of the assets of these organizations grew from approximately $2 trillion to more than $3 trillion. Further, most recent figures show reported annual revenues for Internal Revenue Code (Code) Section 501(c)(3) organizations at $897 billion.

Abuse of Charitable Status Reduces Donor Confidence   Commissioner Everson commented that although the vast majority of nonprofits are conducting their operations in a manner consistent with their missions, some nonprofits are abusing their status as charities.

> If these abuses are left unchecked, I believe there is the risk that Americans not only will lose faith in and reduce support for charitable organizations, but that the integrity of our tax system also will be compromised. I am committed to combating abuse in this area. We recently released our IRS Strategic Plan for 2005–2009. Along with improving service and modernizing our computer systems, one of our strategic goals is to enhance enforcement of the tax law . . . .

In recent years there have been a number of very prominent and damaging scandals involving corporate governance of publicly traded organizations. The Sarbanes-Oxley Act has addressed major concerns about the interrelationships between a corporation, its executives, its accountants and auditors, and its legal counsel. Although Sarbanes-Oxley was not enacted to address issues in tax-exempt organizations, these entities have not been immune from leadership failures. We need go no further than our daily newspapers to learn that some charities and private foundations have their own governance problems. Specifically, we have seen business contracts with related parties, unreasonably high executive compensation, and loans to executives. We at the IRS also have seen an apparent increase in the use of tax-exempt organizations as parties to abusive transactions. All these reflect potential issues of ethics, internal oversight, and conflicts of interest . . . .[5]

Enhancing Nonprofit Governance   The testimony emphasized that stronger governance procedures are needed for exempt organizations.

The sanctions for serious lapses in governance are clear. There is the possibility of revocation of exemption, along with the various excise taxes against individuals that I mentioned before. But sanctions are a last resort. Organizations without effective governance controls are more likely to have compliance problems . . . [The IRS will] require disclosure of whether the organization has a conflict-of-interest policy or an independent audit committee, and whether additional disclosure should be required concerning certain financial transactions or insider relationships. [The IRS] Form 990 revision team is working on a comprehensive overhaul of the form to provide better compliance information about these organizations to the IRS, the states, and the public.

IRS Strategic Plan for 2005 to 2009   The commissioner assured the Finance Committee that the IRS Strategic Plan sets out four key objectives designed to enhance tax law enforcement over the next five years. One of these objectives directly addresses the charitable sector. That objective is to deter abuse within tax-exempt and governmental entities and misuse of such entities by third parties for tax avoidance and other unintended purposes.

Growth in the IRS Budget   As further evidence of the Executive Branch's commitment to supporting the IRS in its more aggressive oversight of the nonprofit sector, the commissioner reported that despite the importance of this sector, "until recently our enforcement budget was not keeping up with its growth. By September [2005] we will see a *thirty (30) percent increase in enforcement personnel for Exempt Organizations over September 2003 levels*" (emphasis added).

Lack of Nonprofit Compliance   In one of his most powerful statements, the commissioner cited a number of factors that are impacting compliance in the tax-exempt area.

> As might be expected, these factors do not necessarily operate independently of one another. Taken together, however, they add up to a *culture that has become more casual about compliance and less resistant to non-compliance*. These are attitudes that we [the IRS and Congress] must work together to change. *An independent, empowered, and active board of directors is the key to insuring that a tax-exempt organization serves public purposes, and does not misuse or squander the resources in its trust* (emphasis added).

Collaborative Enforcement Activities with Other Federal Agencies   Commissioner Everson said that the IRS is working with other federal agencies in a number of areas. "For example, [the IRS] continues to engage in information sharing with the FTC [Federal Trade Commission] to learn more about the credit counseling industry . . . . We expect to continue this mutually beneficial relationship and find other ways to leverage our scarce resources."[6]

Quality and Timeliness of Filing of Form 990   The IRS will be looking at "organizations that failed to, or did not fully complete, compensation information on Form 990. This information will help inform the IRS about current practices of self-governance, both best practices and compliance gaps, and will help us focus our examination program to address specific problem areas," said Commissioner Everson.

Improving Form 990   The IRS has recognized that the current 990 form is not particularly

> "user-friendly," and does not give us all the information IRS agents need to do their jobs; the public is similarly constrained. We are at work revising the

form. [The IRS] anticipates that the revised form will have specific questions or even separate schedules that focus on certain problem areas. For example, filers should not be surprised to find specific schedules or detailed questions relating to credit counseling activities, supporting organizations, compensation practices, and organizational governance. The timing of the revision of the Form 990 is somewhat dependent on our partners, including the states which use the Form 990 as a state filing, and software developers. We are also expanding our Form 990 imaging capabilities. [The IRS] already images the returns of public charities and private foundations . . . for the first time, [the IRS] is imaging the returns of our many categories of exempt organizations that are not section 501(c)(3) organizations. This will allow [the IRS] agents immediate access to these returns, and will allow us to respond quickly to public requests for returns. While important at this time, it is our hope that imaging will become a relic of the past as electronic filing becomes the norm.

Vehicle Donations   Commissioner Everson noted:

For a taxpayer, donating a car to a charity has definite appeal. One can help a charitable cause, dispose of the car, and take advantage of tax provisions that are designed to support the generosity of Americans. Deductions are limited to the fair market value of the property. In its recent study, the GAO estimated that about 4,300 charities have vehicle donation programs. In its review of returns for tax year 2000, the GAO estimated that about 733,000 taxpayers claimed deductions for donated vehicles they valued at $500 or more. Highly troubling is GAO's analysis of 54 specific donations, where it appears that the charity actually received less than 10% of the value claimed on the donor's return in more than half the cases, and actually lost money on some vehicles . . . . [The IRS] cannot ignore the clear implications of the study . . . [and] is educating donors and charities on what constitutes a well-run donation program . . . . [The IRS] will be partnering with the states to distribute the brochures to the fundraising community, as the states regulate fundraising activity.[7]

Strong Support for the Eight Guiding Principles of Accountability and Governance from the Independent Sector's 2005 Report   Commissioner Everson commended the Independent Sector and the Panel on the Nonprofit Sector for their role in encouraging adherence to these standards of excellence: "Good governance and accountability are important given the size and impact of the tax-exempt sector in our economy. . . . Total assets of these organizations approximated $3.7 trillion in 2002, with revenues of $1.2 trillion. Collectively these organizations file more than 800,000 annual returns."[8]

Nonprofit Boards: Current Legislative Environment   Commissioner Everson continued:

> Unfortunately, the nonprofit community has not been immune from recent trends toward bad corporate practices. Like their for-profit brethren, many charitable boards appear to be lax in certain areas. Many of the situations in which we have found otherwise law-abiding organizations to be off-track stem from the failure of fiduciaries to appropriately manage the organization. . . . We have found issues relating to how executive compensation is set and reported by nonprofits. Similarly, issues exist as to whether sufficient due diligence and care is taken in filing tax and information returns.

Improved Transparency in the Tax-Exempt Sector   Commissioner Everson reported a positive development in recent years: the improvement in "transparency" within the tax-exempt sector.

> "Transparency" refers to the ability of outsiders—donors, the press, and interested members of the public—to review data concerning the finances and operations of a tax-exempt organization. By creating a means by which the public may review and monitor the activities of tax-exempt organizations, we promote compliance, help preserve the integrity of the tax system, and help maintain public confidence in the charitable sector. To achieve these goals, we began in the mid-to-late 1990s to image Forms 990, the annual information returns filed by many tax-exempt organizations. We put this information on CDs, and provide it to members of the public, including a number of watchdog groups that monitor charitable organizations. These groups put the information up on their websites, where it is available to the press and to the public. This process has resulted in increased press and public scrutiny of the tax-exempt sector, which we believe is highly desirable. It has also increased the ability of the IRS and state regulators to access Form 990 data, because they are more readily available. Transparency is a lynchpin of compliance within the sector. Therefore, part of our work is to improve exempt organization transparency, including better data quality and better data availability. With our e-filing initiatives, planned changes to Form 990, expanded imaging of returns, and changes to the application process

and the Form 1023, we expect substantial progress toward this goal. All exempt organizations can now file their annual returns electronically. Electronic filing was available for Form 990 and 990EZ filers in 2004, and is now available this year for private foundations, which file Form 990-PF. We want to encourage e-filing because it reduces taxpayer errors and omissions and allows us, and ultimately the public, to have ready access to the information on the return. For this reason, we have required e-filing in certain cases. Under proposed and temporary regulations, by 2007 we will require electronic filing for larger public charities and all private foundations.

What This Means for Nonprofit Boards

The reports, testimony, recommendations, and legislation from the federal and state governments all point to significant changes in the way nonprofits operate. The most important change, however, is the increased level of accountability and transparency that nonprofit boards must accept in their dealings. The IRS commissioner emphasized that "an independent, empowered, and active board of directors is the key to insuring that a tax-exempt organization serves public purposes, and does not misuse or squander the resources in its trust."[9] In a similar vein, the Grassley White Paper recommended that:

> The Board must establish basic organizational and management policies and procedures of organization and review any proposed deviations. The Board must establish, review, and approve program objectives and performance measures and, review and approve significant transactions. The Board must review and approve the auditing and accounting principles and practices used in preparing the organization's financial statements and must retain and replace the organization's independent auditor. An independent auditor must be hired by the Board and each such auditor may be retained only five years. The Board must review and approve the organization's budget and financial objectives as well as significant investments, joint ventures, and business transactions. The Board must oversee the conduct of the corporation's business and evaluate whether the business is being properly managed.
>
> The Board must establish a conflicts of interest policy (which would be required to be disclosed with the 990), and require a summary of conflicts determinations made during the 990 reporting year. The Board must establish and oversee a compliance program to address regulatory and liability concerns.[10]

The proposals for reform indicate that the traditional legal standards of care, loyalty, and obedience will very likely be incorporated into a law governing board member behavior. The proposals clearly indicate that the board is regarded as the final authority in the management of the nonprofit organization and, as such, will be held accountable for the implementation of a conflict-of-interest policy and whistleblower protection. The Grassley White Paper also recommends that the IRS should have the authority to require the removal of any board member, officer, or employee of an exempt organization who has been found to have violated self-dealing rules, conflicts of interest, excess benefit transaction rules, private inurement rules, or charitable solicitation laws. The IRS may require that such an individual may not serve on any other exempt organization for a period of years. An organization that knowingly retained a person who is not so permitted to serve would lose tax exempt status or be subject to a lesser penalty.

Moving the Board into the Twenty-First Century

In a 2003 speech, New York Attorney General Eliot Spitzer directed pointed comments at [nonprofit] board members, identifying lack of board member participation as the largest problem within the nonprofit community.

"The reason many people sit on the boards of not-for-profits is because they've been donors. They believe in the mission," Spitzer said. "But, too often after being appointed to the board, people don't appreciate their responsibility," he charged. J. Cynthia Weber, a development consultant with Girl Scouts of the USA in New York City, was impressed by Spitzer's comments. She said it has been assumed for too long that the moral goodness of mission equates to pureness of execution, which is not always the case.

Spitzer's comments reflect a growing public concern about charitable accountability, said Bennett Weiner, chief operating officer of BBB Wise Giving Alliance, a watchdog group in Arlington, Virginia.[11]

At issue is the level of competence, accountability, and transparency within nonprofit boards. Some nonprofit boards have been collections of friends, business acquaintances, and even family members. Prior public scrutiny and expectations regarding nonprofit boards was low, as IRS Commissioner Everson noted at the Grassley Hearings. Until now federal agencies, such as the Internal Revenue Service, simply did not have the resources or the directive to pursue nonprofit compliance. In the past nonprofit board members were expected to provide a rubber stamp of approval for the executive director and raise money if necessary. Often the members' personal checkbooks were the main source in the nonprofit's fundraising strategy. All that has changed. The number of prominent nonprofits embroiled in financial scandal has increased dramatically. With the enactment of SOX in relation to corporate scandal, the public is demanding that the nonprofit world be held to the same level of accountability to protect the billions of voluntary donations that pour into this sector each year.

Expectations of Board Accountability

What Board Members in Corporations and Nonprofits Have Always Been Expected to Do   All boards, nonprofit and private sector alike, have always had standards of behavior associated with membership. The quality of board decisions and actions are evaluated based on how board members understood their obligations to the nonprofit institution and how carefully they deliberated before making a particular decision/action. Board members are expected to conduct themselves and make decisions consistent with three legal standards: care, loyalty, and obedience. The three standards describe the types of consideration that should go into behavior and decisions. The basic legal standard of the "reasonably prudent person" is particularly significant as the courts look to determine if a board took reasonable steps in decision making or action. Exhibit 2.1 summarizes these standards and the expected impact on board member behavior.

Nonprofit board members have always been expected to attend board meetings on a regular basis. Board members who do not attend meetings regularly have only a marginal understanding of the nonprofit's operational, financial, and governance issues. These members make poor representatives of the nonprofit and, in their lack of knowledge, can make unwise decisions. Board members have always been expected to understand and act on their governance role. They are expected to put the welfare of the nonprofit ahead of any personal consideration, and certainly ahead of any personal gain. Board members are not there as "window dressing" for the benefit of senior management's agenda.

EXHIBIT 2.1   STANDARDS SUMMARY

Legal Standard	Expected Behavior
Care	The director shall discharge his or her duties as a director, including his or her duties as a member of a committee, in good faith and with a care that an ordinarily prudent person in a like position would exercise under similar circumstances, and in a manner the director reasonably believes to be in the best interest of the organization.
Loyalty	In his or her capacity as a member of a nonprofit board, the individual is to give first priority to the institution in making financial decisions. This means that board members may not engage in activities with the nonprofit that will result in personal gain, nor are board members to use their board status as means to any personal gain—financial or otherwise.
Obedience	Directors are required to act within the bounds of the law generally, and with the intent of achieving the organization's mission as expressed in its charter and bylaws.

Board members have always been expected to go to meetings prepared to discuss the matters on the agenda. They were expected to read and understand (or ask questions until they obtain clarity) all materials sent in advance of a board meeting. The operative expectation is that board members come to board meetings *prepared* to ask questions or obtain clarity because they have carefully reviewed all of the materials in advance. Board members have always been obliged to review financial documents carefully and provide appropriate oversight. They are expected either to understand the financial documents or to seek assistance in learning how to read and interpret financial statements. In the area of financial operations, board members need to ask the difficult questions and insist on appropriate financial materials.

As part of their fiduciary obligations, board members are required to disclose any real or potential conflicts of interest. The rest of the board needs to know about these real or potential conflicts so that steps can be taken to eliminate their impact on board deliberations and decisions. Similarly, board members need to adhere to a code of ethics that spells out the nonprofit's values and principles. Adherence to a code of ethics is another way in which board members put the interest and well-being of the nonprofit ahead of their own. Exhibit 2.2 presents a legal standards checklist for board members.

EXHIBIT 2.2   BOARD MEMBER LEGAL
STANDARDS CHECKLIST

Legal Standard of Care

☐ Are board members furnished with financial statements and other materials well in advance of the board meetings?

☐ Is an agenda prepared and followed for each board meeting?

☐ Are minutes kept for each board meeting?

☐ Do board members come to the meetings prepared to discuss the issues on the agenda?

☐ Is there a specific decision-making process, such as a specific length of time for discussion followed by a vote?

☐ If a topic needs to be deferred for a vote at a later date, are there specific steps and/or information that will be gathered so that the board can take a vote when the topic is revisited?

Legal Standard of Loyalty

☐ Are board members required to complete a conflict-of-interest letter on an annual basis?

☐ Does the board have specific protocols to handle conflicts of interest as they occur?

☐ Are board members fully briefed (usually at an orientation) about their fiduciary obligations?

☐ Are board members required to sign a code of ethics, and are they held accountable for conducting themselves in accordance with the code?

Legal Standard of Obedience

☐ Are board members briefed on the nonprofit's mission and how that mission is affected by board decisions?

☐ Are board members briefed on the correlation between their decision making and their fiduciary obligations as these impact the nonprofit's mission?

☐ Are board members briefed on the correlation between the quality of their performance and the nonprofit's mission?

New Expectations of Board Accountability   "Accountability" is an important maxim in today's nonprofit governance environment. The media is filled with examples of financial mismanagement, violation of federal employment law, and failure even to conduct due diligence in outsourcing functions. The days of the fully accountable, fully present, "hands-on" board are here to stay.

When a nonprofit encounters crisis scenarios, such as embezzlement of funds or other criminal actions, the board is often the first place to look for the source of the dysfunction. The first question that comes to mind in each of these sad stories is: Where was the board? Did the board understand what was going on? Did the board ignore or condone clearly inappropriate and often criminal behavior? Did the board even know what to look for? Today's boards and board members need to recognize that the level of scrutiny and accountability aimed at nonprofits has increased. No longer can nonprofit boards afford to deal at arm's length with the nonprofit.

The actions of the board and the products of governance have become central issues in SOX legislation, California legislation, and any potential clone legislation because nonprofit boards hold the ultimate accountability for what transpires within the confines of a nonprofit organization. There are *no* excuses for nonprofit board members not to understand what is going on in the organization, nor are there any excuses for board members not holding the executive director accountable for the actions of his or her staff.

Board's New Governance Role   The SOX legislation ushered in a new accountability based on a set of expected outcomes. This section outlines the types of best practices that emerged from the SOX legislation and how these would work for your nonprofit board.

Sarbanes-Oxley legislation requires boards to ensure that a:

- Whistleblower protection policy is in place and enforced
- Document preservation policy exists that contains a prohibition against destroying documents during an investigation or litigation

These best practices will serve to strengthen your board and nonprofit:

- *Board recruitment and retention.* Today's nonprofit boards cannot afford to be populated with individuals who are passive and/or lack the requisite skills—and assertiveness—to provide appropriate governance and oversight to the nonprofit.
- *Audit committee.* Nonprofit boards need to have a separate audit committee that includes at least one board member who is a financial expert. The audit committee must ensure that auditors are not also engaging in additional services, such as consulting, for the nonprofit. The committee is also responsible for ensuring that either the auditing

firm is rotated every three to five years or that the lead auditor is rotated off the nonprofit's audit every three to five years. The members of the audit committee need to be independent board members, not also members of senior management.

- *Financial literacy.* More rigorous review of financial statements and transactions is required. Financial literacy for all board members means that the nonprofit may need to establish a training program to ensure that all members of the board understand how to read and interpret financial reports. The executive director and chief financial officer (CFO) need to be able to certify the accuracy of financial documents and other submissions, such as Form 990s. All members of the board must be fully aware of the financial condition of the organization, and the executive director and the CFO must be able to sign forms and financial reports without hesitation.

- *Code of ethics for board and senior management; prohibition against inside dealings.* The board needs to adopt a policy strictly prohibiting personal loans to any director or officer and a human resources policy that prohibits lending money to the CEO, executive director, CFO, or other staff. This policy describes the types of behavioral expectations that relate to the roles of board member and member of senior management. One provision that is particularly significant is the prohibition against any type of loan or financial gift by the nonprofit to a board member or member of the staff at any level. No exceptions should *ever* be made to these policies.

- *Conflict-of-interest policy.* Why is not disclosing a conflict of interest a violation of this legal standard? Contrary to what many nonprofit board members believe, disclosing that you may have a potential conflict of interest is not a crime against humanity! A conflict of interest is simply that—the situation can, if ignored, establish conflicting interests between the board member and the nonprofit. The individual board member is not "guilty" of anything by disclosing that he or she has a potential conflict of interest. Actually, this type of disclosure is something to be applauded. The important next step is to have the potential conflict of interest documented via a "Conflict-of-Interest Statement" that all board members and senior staff should submit annually or in the event that they learn of a potential conflict of interest.

- *Decision-making models.* Board members need to understand that they are expected to participate fully in decision making. To facilitate productive discussion and efficient use of time, board leadership can institute ground rules to control the length of time that any one person has the floor, civility of discussion, and the use of a "timed" agenda and Robert's Rules of Order to ensure an orderly meeting. Premeeting preparedness is an essential element to any successful meeting. Board members need to receive materials at least one week prior to a meeting. The process can be streamlined by sending materials as e-mail attachments or by fax. Regardless of the means of conveying the materials, the board members must come to the meeting prepared to deliberate/make decisions. A functional decision-making model also presumes a board culture that supports asking difficult questions and making businesslike decisions. Nonprofits can no longer afford to have otherwise competent professionals on their boards who are permitted to abdicate their governance obligations because they sit on a nonprofit board.

Benefits of Best Practices

- *Improved quality and productivity of board meetings.* One of the challenges in board deliberations is the tendency to engage in endless analytic exercises. Reports from standing committees or ad hoc groups should include recommendations based on solid analysis. The board should request the level of information that is necessary and sufficient for reasonable decision making. The meeting agenda should outline the decisions that are to be made at the meeting, allocate sufficient time for discussion, and then call a vote. Board members who wish to commandeer the agenda tend to use lengthy discussion as a strategic weapon. In this way, the important issues never come up for a vote. The board leadership needs to be assertive in ensuring that the agenda is balanced and that the necessary votes are taken.

- *Board leadership and role clarity.* Board members, particularly board officers, have an obligation to the organization, its staff, clients, volunteers, donors, and the community at large to conduct themselves in a professional manner while acting in their role as board members. The good name of the organization can be enhanced or compromised depending on how they conduct themselves: in person, in print (letters or documents), and online via e–mail.

- *Governance and oversight.* The Senate Finance Committee's staff proposals and California's Nonprofit Integrity Act are based on the presumption that nonprofit boards have established policies to set goals and objectives for the organization as well as protocols to oversee the nonprofit's operations, particularly financial operations. The Senate Finance Committee staff proposals emphasize a significantly higher expectation of board accountability by proposing criminal liability for failing to ensure that the CEO was provided reasonable assurance of the accuracy and completeness of all material aspects of the return. The board is the final authority in the nonprofit and is obligated to closely supervise its only employee, the Chief Executive Officer.

Board's Overall Responsibility for the Management of the Nonprofit

Traditional board responsibilities have always established the board as the ultimate authority in the nonprofit. In addition to the principles that have emerged from the current legislative environment, boards need to ensure that they operate in a manner consistent with traditional practices regarding board authority and overall responsibility for nonprofit management. Boards are responsible for crafting the procedures, policies, and protocols that ensure the nonprofit is a viable entity that is in compliance with federal, state, and local laws. The board's fiduciary obligations also require careful oversight of financial operations to ensure that a budget is crafted on an annual basis, that an annual audit or financial review is conducted, and that IRS Form 990s are submitted in a timely fashion. The board is also responsible for ensuring that all other financial reports are generated in a timely fashion. The board needs to ensure that documentation of its actions and board minutes are prepared in the appropriate manner and stored per the document preservation policy.

The board should ensure that human resource policies are in place to safeguard the rights of employees and volunteers and to make certain that every employee and volunteer has a job description and a method by which his or her performance is evaluated appropriately and fairly. The board should also ensure that the nonprofit publishes both an employee manual and a volunteer manual that identify and outline policies that apply to those individuals.

The board, as the ultimate authority in the nonprofit, is responsible for ensuring that the nonprofit is adequately insured, including the variety of insurance policies that are required for the nonprofit's operations, professional liability coverage (if applicable), and directors and officers insurance, including Employment Practices Liability Insurance for the board. The board is also responsible for ensuring that this coverage is secured at a competitive price and that the nonprofit's insurance professional is responsive to the organization's needs and requirements.

WHY DO NONPROFIT BOARDS HAVE DIFFICULTY IN ADJUSTING TO TWENTY-FIRST-CENTURY EXPECTATIONS?

Tradition, Congress, the Internal Revenue Service, and even Governor Schwarzenegger have spelled out what is expected of nonprofit boards in the twenty-first century. Why do nonprofit boards have difficulty adjusting to this new level of accountability? The difficulties relate to the:

- Corporate culture of nonprofits
- Outdated and nonproductive working paradigm of boards
- Entitlement mentality
- Boards lack of human and intellectual capital to lead effectively
- Denial

Corporate Culture

Board members believe that "nonprofits are different" and should not be held to the same level of accountability as private-sector firms. Small and not-so-small nonprofits claim that compliance costs too much money. Nonprofit management contends that they cannot afford it and believe that the board cannot force management to change.

Outdated and Unproductive Working Paradigms

Nonprofits sometimes generate a litany of woes to justify their indolent behavior. Nonprofit mantras often reflect an organizational culture of economic martyrdom—they work so hard and do not get paid that much. Nonprofit executives sometimes use the same rationale for refusing to demand accountability and performance because the salary structure is below market. Another version of the culture of economic martyrdom is the poverty mentality, which emphasizes that the nonprofit's clients are poor people, so conducting operations in a professional manner is tantamount to selling out to the Establishment.

Entitlement Mentality

On the opposite end of the argument is the board or management's entitlement mentality. Board members may feel that their social or business positions require them to sit on boards to fulfill a kind of *noblesse oblige* obligation or to achieve a level of social visibility in the community. Many nonprofit boards conduct a social hour, not a board meeting. Meetings rarely contain serious deliberations or attention to policy delineation.

Board Lacks Human and Intellectual Capital to Lead Effectively

A nonprofit board's reluctance to join the twenty-first century can be tied to mediocre methods of board member recruitment. Board members are told "there isn't much to do" because the nonprofit believes that lowering performance expectations and quality standards will attract board members. These boards are convinced that there simply are not any people who would willingly join a nonprofit board to accept a challenging assignment. These are the same boards that are unwilling to make a commitment to spend the time and money to hire and retain the best executive director for their organization; nor are they willing to actively supervise the executive director.

Denial

Despite all of the data to the contrary, there are still boards that believe SOX, the California Nonprofit Integrity Act, and other possible state legislation do *not really apply to them.* They continue to labor under the delusion that it is just a bad dream will go away someday. It will all go away the day that donors stop caring about whether their donations are being used

EXHIBIT 2.3   COSTS OF DYSFUNCTION
IN YOUR BOARD

Board Recruitment and Retention
- Has the board experienced difficulty in recruiting individuals with excellent credentials and specific skill sets to the board?
- Has the board lost individuals whose skill sets were important to the nonprofit?
- Have board members expressed dissatisfaction with their board experience?

Decision Making
- Are decisions delayed or stymied by endless discussion, committee meetings, or other methods?
- Are there metrics in place to establish objectives before making a decision?
- Are the appropriate players involved in the discussion? If the discussion entails only lower-level staff who have no authority to make a decision, then the process is dysfunctional.
- How are the relevant facts and data gathered prior to making a decision?
- How are decisions evaluated? Is there a mechanism for reviewing important decisions to determine if a course correction is needed?

Insurance Premiums and Availability
- Has the nonprofit experienced difficulty obtaining insurance at the appropriate limits for a competitive price?
- Has the nonprofit experienced a large number of claims? Major claims? Claims in one particular area?
- Are supervisors held accountable for the frequency and severity of on-the-job injuries? Has the nonprofit's worker's compensation experience modification increased in the past three years?

Difficulty in Attracting Major Donors, Grants and Other Sources of Capital
- Has the nonprofit had difficulty in securing major gifts from donors? If so, what reasons have the donors given for declining to give a major gift?
- Has the nonprofit been turned down for grants or other project-related funding?
- Has the nonprofit had difficulty obtaining a line of credit, mortgage, or other loan products?

Programs and Clients
- Have current programs been reviewed to determine if they are still relevant and providing the types of services that your clients need?
- Do programs have eligibility requirements? How might potential clients learn if they are eligible for a program?
- Is there an appeal process for individuals who would like services from the nonprofit but were denied service because they didn't meet specific criteria?

Regulators
- Has the nonprofit received inquiries from the Internal Revenue Service and/or any state of federal regulators about its operations?
- Has the nonprofit been named in any complaints to governmental agencies?

as they were intended, when citizens stop sending Senator Grassley information about nonprofits that have misappropriated funds to support an executive director's lifestyle, and when we stop reading about nonprofit scandals in the newspapers. Exhibit 2.3 summarizes the costs of board dysfunction.

SUMMARY

The requirements of Sarbanes-Oxley legislation, the new emphasis on enforcement by the Internal Revenue Service, and the provisions of state legislation all address *responsibilities that have always existed in nonprofit governance*. Nonprofit boards have always been expected to understand that they are ultimately accountable for whatever happens in the nonprofit. Nonprofit boards have always been expected to conduct operations in a responsible, conscientious, and transparent fashion. There is nothing new or difficult in the SOX requirements, best practices, IRS regulations, or California's Nonprofit Integrity Act. These obligations have always been in place but have been ignored by people who do not act in the nonprofit's best interest.

ENDNOTES

1. Williams 2005.
2. Fain 2005.
3. Grassley 2005.
4. *San Francisco Chronicle* 2005.
5. Everson 2004.
6. Everson 2004.
7. Everson 2004.
8. Everson 2005.
9. Everson 2004.
10. Grassley White Paper, June 2004.
11. Jones 2003.

CHAPTER 3

Leveraging Sarbanes-Oxley Requirements and Best Practices to Move Your Board to a Higher Level of Performance

Several members of a nonprofit board, including the chair, have gathered for a meeting to discuss an array of topics. The most volatile of the topics is the conflict-of-interest issues that one of the members has encountered in his committee work. The incidents he encountered in the previous months were very serious. One of nonprofit A's staff members sits on the board of nonprofit B, which is a vendor to nonprofit A. Contractors who currently provide services to nonprofit A were seated as voting members on the committee that authorized their contracts. These conflicts were so blatant that they needed immediate action. The board member reported that management's reaction to his identifying this situation bordered on hostility. The member insisted that the chair take action. As a risk manager, this board member pointed out that dealing with conflicts of interest is significant in Sarbanes-Oxley compliance and best practices. The chair emphatically stated, "Sarbanes-Oxley has nothing to do with nonprofits! You don't know what you are talking about!"

WHAT ARE THE SOX REQUIREMENTS AND BEST PRACTICES?

When a nonprofit faces a crisis, the board is often the first place to look for the source of the dysfunction. The first question that comes to mind when a nonprofit finds itself in a dilemma is "Where was the board?" Did the board understand what was going on? Did the board ignore or condone clearly inappropriate and often criminal behavior? Did the board even know what to look for? Today's boards and board members need to recognize that the level of scrutiny and accountability aimed at nonprofits has increased. Nonprofit boards can no longer afford to deal at arm's length with the organization—or meet on a quarterly basis, as was once touted in a well-known governance model. The days of the fully accountable, fully present, "hands-on" board are here to stay.

The actions of the board and the products of governance have become central issues in SOX legislation, California legislation, and any other potential clone legislation because nonprofit boards hold the ultimate accountability for what transpires within the confines of a nonprofit organization. There are no excuses for nonprofit board members not to understand what is going on in the organization, nor are there any excuses for board members not to hold the executive director accountable for the actions of his or her staff.

Who Is Watching Your Nonprofit?

The misguided chair in the story may think that Sarbanes–Oxley has nothing to do with nonprofits, but she is wrong. Nonprofits are subject to a higher level of public scrutiny than ever before. Important and visible agencies, regulators, advocates as well as the media are examining nonprofit accountability and transparency.[1]

The Media   Public opinion of the nonprofit world is often influenced by the types of nonprofit scandals people read about or hear dissected on cable television. "It was as if the charitable sector was made of Velcro—virtually every scandal worked its will in converting what had been benign, soft opinion into increasingly negative, hard attitudes."[2] Nonprofits that believe that they will never be subjected to any sort of media scrutiny are deluding themselves. Any colleges, universities, or other types of academic institutions that believe that the media could not possibly be interested in their operations need only review the almost daily coverage of the American University scandal in the *Washington Post* and the *Chronicle of Philanthropy* and other print media. The coverage went on for weeks. Television and radio coverage can be equally persistent. The ever-present cameras and live video capacity can make even the smallest story headline news if the timing is right. The media outlets are present in every major city and can arrive virtually anywhere within hours.

Appearance of impropriety, whether such impropriety really exists or not, is still damaging to the public trust that a nonprofit enjoys.

Internal Revenue Service   The commissioner of the Internal Revenue Service, Mark Everson, made a commitment to higher scrutiny of the nonprofit sector in his testimony before the Senate Finance Committee in 2004 and 2005. Evidence of this commitment is demonstrated in the announcement by Martha Sullivan, the head of the IRS office that oversees tax-exempt groups, that her department has hired 105 auditors in recent months as part of a "cultural shift" toward stricter and more thorough enforcement of the laws governing nonprofit organizations."[3]

Federal Government—Senate Finance Committee   Appendix A contains the letter that was sent by Senator Charles Grassley, chair of the Senate Finance Committee, to Thomas Gottschalk, acting chair of the board of American University. The senator's letter requested a wide array of documents, including:

- Benjamin Ladner's compensation package, as well as materials utilized by the board in approving the package
- A list of no-bid contracts over $100,000 for the 11 years that Ladner was president of American University
- Proof that the board was in compliance with its state fiduciary duties in its actions regarding the hiring, retention, compensation of, and termination of Ladner.
- IRS filings and correspondence for the past five years

The intent of Senator Grassley's inquiry was to determine the degree to which the board was complicit, by their inaction, in the university president's financial mismanagement.

The overarching theme in Senator Grassley's letter is that the board is ultimately accountable for the actions of the nonprofit, for the selection of qualified board members, for the executive's compensation package, and for the proper stewardship of donor funds. This message is explicit in its demand for greater board accountability. Senator Grassley's inquiry is not political grandstanding. The call for nonprofit reform, accountability, and transparency is bipartisan.

Watchdog Groups   One of the more important contributions to the testimony at the 2005 Grassley hearings was from the Better Business Bureau's Wise Giving Alliance president and chief executive, Art Taylor. This group provides guidance to potential donors and tracks evidence of donor apprehension. In 2001 the alliance commissioned Princeton Survey Research Associates International to conduct a major donor expectations survey, the results of which are available on the www.give.org Web site.

Among the key findings of the alliance survey are:

- 70 percent of respondents say it is difficult to know whether a charity is legitimate.
- 44 percent say it is difficult to find the information they want in making a giving decision.
- 50 percent say they would be "very likely" to get information they wanted from the charity itself, although only 50 percent think that the charities provide enough information about their activities to help them decide about giving.
- Donors are not sure what information they need or where they should get it or, in some cases, how to assess the information they have. They are looking for help in finding accountable charities.[4]

The alliance produces reports on national charities that specify whether an organization meets or does not meet the Standards for Charity Accountability. The reports do not rank or grade charities but rather seek to assist donors in making informed judgments about charities soliciting their support. In addition, the alliance goes beyond standards to issue special alerts and advisories for individuals on topics related to giving. These include tips on donating cars as well as tips on charity telemarketing, police and firefighter appeals, and charitable responses to disasters.

In today's world of 24/7 media, e-mail, Internet, and regulatory scrutiny, nonprofits are no longer invisible. It is no longer an option for nonprofit boards to conduct business—or ignore it—in the manner they have always done.

SARBANES-OXLEY REQUIREMENTS

Currently, only two of the provisions in SOX directly apply to nonprofit organizations. Nonprofits are required to adhere to "whistleblower protection" requirements that provide protection to employees who report suspected fraud or other illegal activities. Employees or volunteers of a nonprofit are shielded from retaliation for making reports of waste, fraud, or abuse.

Nonprofits are also expected to have a fully functioning document preservation policy in place. This policy has two aspects: preservation and archiving of documents for the purpose of timely retrieval, and a prohibition against the destruction or falsification of records or documents.

Whistleblower Protection

The first obligation from SOX that applies to all organizations is the requirement for a documented whistleblower protection policy. SOX requires all organizations, including nonprofits, to establish a means to collect, retain, and resolve claims regarding accounting, internal accounting controls, and auditing matters. The system must allow such concerns to be submitted anonymously. SOX provides significant protections to whistleblowers and severe penalties to those who retaliate against them. Policies and procedures (see Appendix B) on whistleblower protection should contain at least these features:

- There is a confidential avenue for reporting suspected waste, fraud, and abuse.
- There is a process to thoroughly investigate any reports.
- There is a process for disseminating the findings from the investigation.
- The employee filing the complaint will not be subjected to termination, firing, or harassment, or miss out on promotion.
- Even if the findings do not support the nature of the complaint, the employee or volunteer who made the complaint will not face any repercussions.

- All employees and volunteers should have a copy of the whistle-blower policy, and it should be posted in clear view. This policy should also be covered in any orientation or training programs the organization offers for its employees and volunteers.

How Does Whistleblower Protection Work in a Nonprofit? There are many ways in which staff, volunteers, and members of a nonprofit convey their sentiments or report problems. Some nonprofits solicit feedback via surveys or suggestion boxes. Other types of feedback are conveyed without being solicited. The spirit and letter of a whistleblower protection policy is that feedback or reports, whether solicited or not, will not subject the sender to any negative consequences. The management of a nonprofit organization need not approve of the content of the report or comment, but cannot subject the person making the report or comment to negative consequences.

The Sunshine Garden Club distributed a survey to its members to evaluate the management quality of the current committee chairs. The club's organizational structure is somewhat complex with several layers of volunteer management under the control of the board. In completing her evaluation, one member, Ann Green, gave high marks to the committee chair, Gwendolyn Brown, but reported that the section chair, Mary Smith, was unsatisfactory in her performance. Mary Smith supervises Gwendolyn Brown. Mary was furious that a member dared to criticize her performance. Mary called Ann and left an irate message on her voice mail insisting that Ann call her back to discuss the comments. Ann sent Mary an e-mail stating that she stood by the comments and refused to discuss it further. Mary continued to send e-mails to Ann until Ann threatened to file a formal complaint with the Sunshine Garden Club's president.

Just having a whistleblower protection policy is not enough. Mary Smith's actions are in violation of the spirit of whistleblower protection. Whistleblower protection needs to be enforced, and the nonprofit's leadership needs to be trained to accept all comments and feedback in a manner that is consistent with the spirit and letter of the law.

How Can the Board Ensure That a Whistleblower Protection Policy Is in Place and Enforced? The Sunshine Garden Club's board would have learned that they needed a whistleblower protection policy if Ann Green had complained about Mary Smith and asked to see the club's policy on whistleblower protection. Confidentiality is the key in developing a process whereby employees and volunteers feel safe in reporting waste, fraud, and abuse—or even inferior leadership. One way a confidential reporting system can be established is to use an ombudsman. Another way would be to use a third-party reporting system that is not connected to the organization.

Ombudsmen are trained to resolve problems and can address complaints brought to them. To be effective, an ombudsman is independent of the organization and the position cannot be terminated for reasons other than failure to perform. Having this type of program in place can go a long way to correct problems as they arise and to meet the SOX requirements.

Another method is the use of third-party anonymous hotlines as a risk-free way to report unethical or illegal activity. With a third-party anonymous hotline, an employee or volunteer can report questionable activities at any time of day or night. The hotlines can handle a variety of reporting issues, such as:

- Accounting irregularities
- Violations of governmental regulations
- Fraud
- Falsification or destruction of organizational records
- Possible workplace violence—reports of threats or menacing behavior
- Discrimination
- Sexual harassment
- Conflicts of interest
- Release of proprietary information, particularly if the information has been removed from the workplace

Board members need to request a copy of the nonprofit's whistleblower protection policy from management. The board also needs to request a copy of the written procedures for filing a report and the written procedures used to conduct an investigation and disseminate the findings. All of these documents should be included in employment and volunteer manuals. Further, if the board is not satisfied that management has implemented this policy properly, it can conduct a survey of staff and volunteers to determine if such a policy is in place and whether they know how to make a report and what to expect once the report is made. If the board chooses this option, board members need to draft and disseminate the survey and collect the responses. Management should not be permitted to have access to the survey or the responses. Exhibit 3.1 presents an overview of the whistleblower protection policy.

Document Management and Preservation Policy

How Can the Board Ensure that a Document Preservation Policy Is in Place and Operational?   Document storage and retention is another area within SOX that applies to all organizations. An important part of this requirement is to institute a policy that prohibits destruction of documents during an inquiry or legal action.

This requirement needs to be tailored to address both paper files and electronic files.

Policies on document preservation should be developed by the board and senior management. Senior management must develop a statement that describes what the document retention policy is and why it is required by law. It is important that the staff and volunteers understand that document

EXHIBIT 3.1   OVERVIEW—WHISTLEBLOWER PROTECTION POLICY

Board's Role
The board needs to review the nonprofit's current whistleblower protection policy and/or direct the executive director to draft this policy immediately. The SOX requirement is in effect right now. If your nonprofit does not have a whistleblower protection policy and an employee claims wrongful termination based on whistleblower activities, your nonprofit could lose in subsequent litigation and be assessed punitive damages (which are *not* covered by insurance) or other sanctions.

The board must ensure that there is a mechanism for staff or volunteers to report retaliatory behavior if they have made a report regarding waste, fraud or abuse. Putting this in place sends a message to both senior management and staff/volunteers that the board is serious about remaining in compliance with this provision of SOX.

Nonprofit Requirements
- A whistleblower protection policy
- A method for reporting waste, fraud or abuse
- Procedures for conducting investigations
- Protocols for disseminating findings (in conjunction with your legal counsel)

See Appendix B for a sample whistleblower protection policy.

preservation is a requirement of SOX and that this requirement applies to all businesses and nonprofits. The policy should also describe the new procedures and the deliverables that the board expects. Expectations of individual performance need to be specified as well as the consequences (for individual employees and volunteers) for failing to adhere to the new procedures. Chapter 7 examines the development and implementation of a document preservation policy.

IMPLEMENTING SOX BEST PRACTICES

In addition to the SOX requirements, the board is expected to implement best practices that have emerged from the other provisions of the SOX legislation. These best practices include:

- *Appointing an audit committee.* The role of this audit committee is to oversee the annual audit or financial review (for small nonprofits) and to upgrade the financial literacy of the board. The audit committee is the link between the board and its auditor or financial reviewer. The audit committee is an important element in ensuring that the board understands the results of the annual audit or financial review (for small nonprofits) and that the board's skills in reading and interpreting financial statements are kept up to date. The intent of this best practice is the complete independence of the auditor and the audit committee. This means that if the person who is currently conducting the nonprofit's audit or financial review also prepares the nonprofit's IRS 990 form, that individual must divest himself or herself from one of these roles. The intent of SOX legislation is to segregate these duties. An auditor or auditing firm that provides services to a nonprofit in addition to conducting an audit presents a conflict of interest.

- *Certifying financial statements.* The nonprofit's board is ultimately accountable for the accuracy and integrity of the nonprofit's financial statements and IRS 990 forms. The board needs to ensure that the nonprofit's executive director, chief executive officer, or chief financial officer can validate the accuracy of the nonprofit's financial statements. "For a nonprofit organization, CEO and CFO sign-off on financial statements would not carry the weight of law [unless it is required under state law], but it would signal the importance that the

CEO, in particular, pays to understanding the nonprofit's financial condition. . . . Signing off on the financial statements provides formal assurance that both the CEO and CFO have reviewed them carefully and stand by them."[5]

Ensuring the accuracy of financial statements begins at board level. Financial oversight is one of the most important aspects of the board's fiduciary responsibilities. Nonprofits, by virtue of their community-minded culture, are particularly vulnerable to fraud by means of an "atmosphere of trust within the organization, a steady stream of cash donations, and a reliance on volunteers to perform important tasks, a limited supervisory resources and unpaid boards of directors with little or no financial expertise."[6]

The audit committee's role is central to ensuring that the board and the nonprofit's senior management live up to their fiduciary obligations. In addition to the audit committee's responsibilities of choosing an auditor and being the liaison between the board and the auditor, the committee has an important duty to facilitate the reporting of waste, fraud, and abuse. As the audit committee works collaboratively with the auditor, instances of questionable practices or potential fraud may very well be uncovered. The audit committee is tasked with bringing this information to the attention of the board and ensuring that necessary changes are made to ensure the integrity and accuracy of the nonprofit's financial practices and subsequent reports.

The following Sarbanes-Oxley best practices have emerged from Congressional hearings and the White Paper prepared by the Senate Finance Committee staff in June 2004. The point of these best practices is to upgrade the level of accountability and transparency of the nonprofit and its board.

- *Enhanced detail and accuracy* in the preparation of IRS tax documents in the annual submission of IRS 990 filings. Failure to submit a 990 is no longer an option.
- *Instituting a higher level of board accountability*, including upgraded policies and procedures for board member recruitment, board orientation, performance expectations, and adherence to legal principles of governance.
- *Conflict-of-interest policy.* A conflict-of-interest policy directly relates to the board's fiduciary obligations. Board members are expected to put

the well-being of the nonprofit at the forefront of any decision. Board members are not permitted to enjoy any financial gain from their membership on the board—even indirectly. This means that they cannot leverage their board membership to obtain contracts for their firm or to earn any form of revenue. Most nonprofit boards, unlike boards in the private sector, do not pay stipends to their members. Having a conflict-of-interest policy in place helps board members focus on decision making for the good of the nonprofit.

- *Code of ethics* for board and senior management that precludes any loans to directors, officers, management, or staff of the nonprofit.
- *Internal controls*, particularly as these relate to financial operations, and compliance with all laws and regulations at the federal, state, and local level.
- *Transparency at all levels of management including the board*, and in all transactions including travel claims and reimbursements. The board needs to insist that there are written procedures for filing travel and reimbursement claims and that these procedures are enforced—even by means of unannounced audits.
- *Consistent adherence to new policies and procedures and enforcement of the policies.* The board will not be successful in its endeavors to bring the nonprofit into compliance unless the new policies and procedures are enforced.

SOX and the Board: Achieving Greater Accountability

SOX best practices relating to governance emphasize the importance of recruiting a board that is the right size for the nonprofit; has the right competencies, skill sets, and understanding of SOX best practices; and has the right attitude/perspective about the its governance role.

Some members of the board may be appropriate to the organization, while others may be above their heads in terms of understanding their role and what is expected of them. SOX best practices presumes that all members of the board are qualified to serve—that is, competent to serve in a governance role—and possess an understanding of what is expected of them as well as a skill set that serves to accomplish expected performance.

Boards must recognize their fundamental obligation of "active independent and informed oversight" of the nonprofit's affairs, including overseeing senior management. Boards need to be independent; the majority of the board's members should not be part of senior management and other relationships in both fact and appearance. The board is well advised to define in its governance documents "independence" in the context of its particular charitable mission. For a director to be regarded as independent, the board should confirm conclusively that the director has no material relationship that would create a "risk of bias."[7]

In order to move forward in today's legal environment, the board should establish practices that:

- Connect deliberations and activities to the organization's charitable mission.
- Develop a basic statement of the director's duties and responsibilities, including expectations regarding time commitment.
- Establish qualifications for board membership, including diversity of experience, skills, and other related qualifications that must be in place before a prospective member is seated on the board.
- Provide director orientation, continuing education, and evaluation requirements.
- Establish performance objectives for board committees that carefully delineate the responsibilities and authority of each committee.
- Assure provision of timely and sufficient information. Receiving timely, substantive information in a useful format is crucial for trustees if they are to make informed decisions. This in turn requires (a) a regular board meeting schedule with detailed agendas distributed in advance containing limited "consent" actions and (b) firm adherence to specific attendance requirements and access to senior executives in addition to the CEO as well as to outside advisors. The board should evaluate the adequacy of this information flow process periodically.
- Meet in executive sessions. The governance protocols should require the board to meet in regularly scheduled executive sessions that do not include the CEO or any senior managers. Although this may be politically sensitive, there is a near-universal agreement in the post

Sarbanes-Oxley environment that such meetings help ensure necessary oversight and evaluation of management.[8]

Role of the Board Orientation

How do board members learn about what is expected of them? One of the best ways of offering a complete introduction to board service is through a comprehensive orientation and subsequent in-service training sessions. The orientation for new members should be crafted to address the important issues and expectations. It should also be held at a time of day that would accommodate most members—and should be approximately 90 minutes to 2 hours long. Topics that are not addressed in the initial orientation can be covered in subsequent in-service sessions. The discussion in Chapter 7 elaborates on the best practices for board orientations.

Benefits of Implementing Best Practices

Although SOX legislation only has two requirements for nonprofits, whistleblower protection and document preservation, there are significant benefits to implementing the best practices that have emerged from this law.

Governance   Compliance begins with the board—the ultimate authority within the nonprofit. Unless it begins with the board, it will not happen! A more effective board has members who understand and adhere to their fiduciary obligations and recognize their responsibility in governing the nonprofit. SOX requirements and best practices can be leveraged as a mechanism for enhancing the professionalism of your nonprofit board.

Accountability   SOX compliance and best practices are now the platinum standard in management—your auditor, bank, and insurance professional expect your nonprofit to implement requirements and best practices. Higher level of management and staff accountability improves overall performance.

Operations   Platinum operating standards translate into establishing effective protocols ensure that the nonprofit remains in compliance with SOX and the nonprofit's industry standards and address future standards

Marketing   A nonprofit that advertises that it adheres to the SOX platinum standard in its operating practices can achieve better competitive positioning because most of its nonprofit competitors have not recognized the significance of adopting SOX best practices platinum.

Strategic Positioning   Adherence to SOX offers a nonprofit greater credibility and ability to attract necessary resources: high-quality board members, sources of capital, donors, or other fund sources. It also enables access to insurance, capital, and other resources to solidify your nonprofit's role in the community and expand for a more solid future.

SUMMARY

Sarbanes-Oxley legislation requires all organizations to have a whistleblower protection policy and a document preservation policy. Additionally, the best practices that have emerged strengthen internal controls and call for higher levels of board accountability and transparency. The requirements and best practices bring innumerable benefits to the board and nonprofit alike. Ironically, all of these practices should have been in place in the nonprofit and corporate world all along.

ENDNOTES

1. Owens 2004.
2. Light 2005.
3. Chronicle of Philanthropy, November 10, 2005.
4. BBB 2003.
5. www.guidestar.org.
6. Owens 2004.
7. Peregrine 2003.
8. Peregrine 2003.

CHAPTER 4

SOX as a Cure for the "Leave Your Brains at the Door" Syndrome

Wendell Smith is the treasurer of the Gulf Coast Spinnaker Society. He is a self-assured businessman who feels he has his fingers on the pulse of the organization. His finance committee is made up of male and female professionals from various fields. Additionally, several of the Spinnaker Society managers are assigned to staff this committee. One of the staff members, Fred, is also a silent partner in his family's copier distributing company. Fred's family's company is the vendor for Spinnaker's copiers. Two board members are also silent partners in companies that do business with the Spinnaker Society. Both of these board members sit on the finance committee.

At this month's finance committee meeting, the topic of vendor contracts was on the agenda. One of the Spinnaker board members, Marjorie, also sits on the finance committee, as does the Spinnaker board chair, Samantha. Marjorie questioned whether Fred should be present during this discussion because one of the contracts being discussed is for the copier contract. Marjorie did not know that two members of the finance committee are also silent partners in companies that do business with the Society. Wendell became irate because Marjorie brought up this topic at the meeting without clearing it with him first. He told Marjorie that Fred is very valuable to Spinnaker and should be allowed to sit in on the discussion. When the discussion turned to renewing the contracts, the copier contract was passed without further question by anyone on the committee. If the copier contract had actually been put out for competitive bid, the Spinnaker Society would have discovered that competing firms could have provided the same services for a lower price. Of course, after Marjorie's reprimand, no one dared suggest that the copier contract be put out for competitive bid. Wendell was satisfied that the well-oiled finance committee machine continued to run smoothly and that his colleagues on the board would not have to be challenged about their business dealings by annoying meddlers.

When Marjorie later checked her e-mail she was shocked to discover that the board chair, Samantha, had sent her a vicious e-mail, not only condemning Marjorie's questioning of a potential conflict of interest but also furiously admonishing her for failing to give higher deference to Wendell in his role as treasurer. E-mail can be a wonderful bit of technology—particularly when it documents a violation of the Sarbanes-Oxley whistleblower protection requirement. Marjorie might very well be tempted to forward this delicious piece of hubris to a friend, family member, or a Spinnaker Society major donor; and who knows where it might be forwarded from there. Board chairs like Samantha may think their position gives them the right to keep other board members in line by verbal abuse and intimidation, but this blatant coercion prevents board members from exercising their fiduciary obligations. It is unlikely that the members of the Spinnaker Society's finance committee ever dare ask the difficult questions or fully participate in board discussions.

BOARD DYSFUNCTION IN TODAY'S NEW LEGISLATIVE ENVIRONMENT

The themes of changing expectations and changing accountability should be very clear from the Senate Finance Committee White Paper and the testimony from the IRS commissioner. Congress, the Internal Revenue Service, and state legislatures are all taking steps to ensure that nonprofit boards are not just held accountable for their actions but, in some cases, are held criminally liable for their actions. The nonprofit world is being forced to wake up and behave like professionals. Boards are being replaced en masse, executive directors are being prosecuted and incarcerated. There's no turning back because donors, the public, and lawmakers are now insisting on the same quality of organizational integrity that has been applied to private sector firms via SOX legislation.

Some of the themes that emerged from the Senate Finance Committee hearings include:

- *Lack of faith results in decreased donations.* "If these abuses [by nonprofit organizations] are left unchecked, I believe there is the risk that Americans not only will lose faith in and reduce support for charitable organizations, but that the integrity of our tax system also will be compromised."[1]

- *Are nonprofits' practices consistent with their 501(c)(3) designation?* Nonprofits will be held accountable for demonstrating that their mission, vision, and practices are consistent with their 501(c)(3) designation.

- *Possible accreditation requirement.* Accreditation and reauthorization may be imposed on all nonprofit organizations.

- *IRS 990 forms.* The IRS will scrutinize Form 990s with greater vigilance. IRS Commissioner Mark Everson testified that the Bush administration authorized funding for more aggressive enforcement of nonprofit compliance. Everson added that in the past, the IRS was reluctant to pursue nonprofits, but given the recent high-profile scandals, the IRS, with the blessing of the administration, has toughened its stance.

- *Higher accountability for nonprofit boards.* Nonprofit boards, as the ultimate authority in a nonprofit organization, will be held accountable for the actions of the senior management and staff. Failure to provide assertive oversight will no longer be tolerated.

The changing regulatory atmosphere indicates that it is not a question of "if" or "when" nonprofits will be under greater scrutiny; the time has already come. Understanding your board's operational paradigm will be crucial in designing the strategies you will need to employ to implement these best practices and move your nonprofit to a platinum operating standard.

What Is the "Leave Your Brains at the Door" Syndrome?

Leave your brains at the door (LYBATD) syndrome describes board members' singular or collective inability to apply their education, training, professional skill set, and/or the requisite intellectual rigor to nonprofit board deliberations, decision making, and governance. Those nonprofit boards that have found themselves in high-profile scandals were certainly *not* populated by stupid people. The individuals who are members of these boards often have stellar professional and academic credentials, including professional designations and licenses. These individuals have been successful enough in their personal and professional lives to have amassed the financial and/or social cachet to be recruited to a nonprofit's board. They should be the wind beneath the nonprofit's wings rather than organizational window dressing.

Common Problems that Can Be Traced to LYBATD Syndrome

LYBATD syndrome is often at core of problems related to management and productivity. Common problems that can be traced to the syndrome include:

- *Failure to provide leadership in setting the ethical tone for the board and the organization.* When members of the board are impervious to their own legal and ethical obligations, it is unlikely that they would be interested in raising the ethical standards of the organization.

- *Excessive executive compensation.* The issue of excessive compensation has been a theme in the IRS commissioner's testimony, the Grassley White Paper, and California's Nonprofit Integrity Act. The issue is *not* the negotiation of a compensation package that is reasonable and in keeping with the executive's performance levels. The issue is the board's permitting the executive and/or management team to be compensated in a manner that is excessive for the budget of the nonprofit, or for the executives' performance levels, or for the clandestine manner in which compensation was negotiated and approved. Any executive compensation package that is presented in detail to the board and not voted on by the full board is at risk for inquiry. LYBATD boards prefer to leave the decision making to the executive committee.

- *Failure to recognize financial mismanagement and conversion.* Boards that leave their brains at the door are not likely to have the foggiest notion about the actual financial status of the nonprofit.

- *Why employment practices liability insurance (EPLI) is now a common attachment to directors and officers (D&O) insurance.* Board members who "leave their brains at the door" are also not likely to know about the nonprofit's hiring, supervision, disciplinary and termination practices. Boards composed of members of this type also do not understand that the organization needs a whistleblower protection policy, sexual harassment policy, and a policy to conduct hiring and accommodation in accordance with the Americans with Disabilities Act (ADA). EPLI is now a common attachment to directors and officers (D&O) liability coverage because boards are being held responsible in wrongful termination litigation.

- *Filing of IRS 990 forms.* When IRS 990 forms are filed inconsistently or in an incomplete fashion, the nonprofit's board is being questioned. Boards with LYBATD syndrome rarely understand about the need to file these forms by the stated deadline and in an accurate and complete fashion.

The spillover effects of a dysfunctional board affect not only the board's work, but the work of the nonprofit's senior management and often the entire nonprofit. Exhibit 4.1 lists those effects.

Why Is LYBATD a Common Phenomenon in Nonprofit Boards?

It is baffling to see that individuals who approach their business life and decisions in a rigorous manner appear to do just the opposite when they attend nonprofit board meetings. Some of the reasons for this atypical behavior include the fact that many board members do not understand the fundamental tenets of organizational citizenship. If board members have heard of organizational citizenship, they believe that it is strictly applicable to the rank and file staff. This lack of understanding of organizational citizenship can be seen in board members who engage in multimillion- or

EXHIBIT 4.1   SPILLOVER EFFECTS OF
BOARD DYSFUNCTION

Dysfunctional Board

- Lack of oversight and direction in governance
- Board clique or senior management making all of the important decisions
- Not living up to legal obligations of care, loyalty, and obedience
- Ignores implementation of SOX requirements and best practices
- Fails to appropriately supervise executive director and management team

Dysfunctional Senior Management

- Potential for fraud and mismanagement of nonprofit
- Fails to provide board with accurate financial reports and other documents
- Can engage in inappropriate or illegal activities in dealing with rank and file, such as sexual harassment or violation of whistleblower protection
- Results in higher operating costs (unemployment insurance, costs of training new employees, worker's compensation, etc.)

---

multibillion-dollar transactions at their place of employment, come to a nonprofit board meeting and cannot seem to comprehend financial reports, cannot seem to ask challenging questions, and cannot insist on rigorous performance levels from management and staff.

This lethargy might also be based on a belief by board members that they are not expected to apply private sector values or practices in a non-profit setting lest the nonprofit be accused of "selling out to the Establishment." These spurious beliefs sometimes emerge from the misplaced zeal of the nonprofit's management and staff in focusing their energy and attention on their "oppressed" clientele or in promoting a "poverty mentality." The board might also believe that nonprofit management and other board members are too creative, high-strung, or otherwise overwhelmed to be expected to perform at the level one would expect to see in the private sector.

Often the fundamental reason for LYBATD syndrome is that the board is in deep denial about the dysfunction or mismanagement that exists within their nonprofit. The founder of the nonprofit might still present and functioning in the organization. This individual is unique in imprinting his or her mark on the organizational culture and notions of citizenship and also steadfast in his or her belief of how the nonprofit should operate. Other reasons can be as simple as the desire to preserve social relationships. The board members are social friends and the nonprofit is just a "charity." A board member could be participating merely to get his photo published in *Town and Country*'s society pages. One of the most common reasons for LYBATD syndrome is that although the board member is a consummate professional in her career, she is a personal friend of the nonprofit's executive director and was recruited by that person to serve on the board. The executive director has another vote in his pocket—end of story.

Symptoms of LYBATD Evidenced in Board Dysfunction

Exhibit 4.2 provides examples of the dysfunctional characteristics found in boards and the corresponding description of the board's culture.

LYBATD syndrome can also be found by examining these problems:

- *Attendance at board meetings is uneven.* Most meetings barely have a quorum. Attendance issues suggest that board members either do not understand or do not care about their governance obligations to the nonprofit.

- *Senior staff members aggressively manage the board meetings, and the discussion is dominated by a few board members and/or senior staff.* Questions are discouraged, and articulated dissent is punished. The board does not take active part in discussion and does not review materials. Effective boards are highly collaborative groups. A red flag should go up when it is clear that one or more board members are "opting out" of the deliberations.

- *The board meetings are highly choreographed, but the content of the agenda is superficial, including endless reports by senior management.* The meeting is a dog-and-pony show meant to convey the consistent message that "all is well—just let those of us on the executive committee handle everything." This scenario is particularly dangerous because those in power are working to manipulate the agenda and the level of participation of the rest of the board. Even more troubling is the fact that the rest of the board does not understand that, in their governance role, they are *required* to know what is going on and are expected to demand to be fully informed.

EXHIBIT 4.2   BOARD DYSFUNCTIONS AND
TYPICAL CULTURE

Board Dysfunction	Description of Board Culture
The board is dominated by leaders who bully and dominate members.	The board is a collection of primarily passive individuals who choose, for whatever reasons, to tolerate being forced into accepting the current leadership.
The board consists of passive board members who have no term limits or obligations and who deal with the organization at arm's length.	Board members do not understand their responsibilities and legal obligations.
The nonprofit executive director fields at least six phone calls a day from board members who want to be updated on operational matters.	The board is micromanaging. The culture of this board is distrust of the senior management. Board members and their leaders do not understand the governance role.
The board president, who has been the president for 20 years, is the nonprofit's biggest donor.	Board culture is one of inertia. Some board members have long-term social ties with each other and see their positions of power on the board as appropriate "payback" for their level of financial contribution.
The board has two tiers of membership. The upper tier consists of socially prominent individuals with money and connections, and the lower tier consists of members who are expected to be "worker bees."	This board's culture emerges from an organization that is socially prominent, but has a constituency that demands to be represented despite the fact that there are few socially prominent individuals within that constituency. The lower tier is expected to "pay their way" for being allowed on the board by contributing or raising a stipulated sum each year, sitting on multiple committees, and being assigned to projects that are time and labor intensive. The upper tier of the board is recruited from that city's "high society," and these board members generally have no committee or project obligations. They are simply expected to lend their name to the organization and make significant financial contributions.

Board Dysfunction	Description of Board Culture
The board's committee system produces no results. The board leadership is visibly passive and allows the senior staff to run the board.	This is the classic "rubber-stamp" board. The culture in this board is one that defers all power to senior management. Board members view their role on the board as "feel good."
The artistic director is the board chair, and his volunteer assistant is the second most powerful person in the organization. The board chair routinely refuses to share with the other board members. The board is window-dressing.	This "checkbook" board is a variation on the classic "rubber-stamp" board. The difference here is that not only are board members expected to be passive, but they are also expected to make significant financial contributions.

- *Everyone on your board does not know how much the executive director makes.* Does the board know what perks the executive director enjoys, what are his or her benefits package including pension, vacation time, and professional development time? If these data are being suppressed or withheld by the executive committee, your board has a problem. Board members should not tolerate the "right to privacy" claim; the executive director is the board's only employee. Board members have the right to know everything an employer would know about an employee.

- *Conflict is suppressed, or endless conflict is used to block business from being conducted.* Behind this symptom is a small group of people who are working hard to forward their own agenda by bullying, intimidating, or publicly humiliating those whose opinions differ. These individuals will create gridlock until their agenda is fulfilled.

- *The board does not have a vision or strategic plan for moving the nonprofit ahead.* Senior staff actively blocks strategic planning. As Yogi Berra observed, "When you come to a fork in the road, take it." If your board and nonprofit do not know where it is headed, consider this a huge red flag.

- *Board members have been in place for over five years.* Does your board have term limits? Are the term limits enforced? It is useless to have term limits if board members are permitted to remain on or have limitless reappointments to the board. How many board members have been

on the board over five years? If the number is greater than two, you
need to do some serious housecleaning and board recruitment.

- *Your board does not have directors and officers insurance and/or employment
  practices liability insurance.* Boards that resist purchasing adequate insurance fail to take their responsibilities of care and loyalty seriously. No
  one should ever join a board that is not adequately insured.

- *Financial statements and documents are not presented in a professional format.*
  Haphazard financial statements should signal the need for serious review of internal controls.

- *Management and staff have ignored the letters that the nonprofit's auditor has
  provided to the board following annual audits.* These management opinions indicate those areas in your nonprofit's financial workings that
  require immediate attention. Although senior management has consistently failed to take necessary action to mitigate those deficiencies,
  the board has not held management accountable or imposed sanctions. In today's environment of higher accountability, this failure by
  the board to live up to its fiduciary obligation could result in legal
  consequences for the board and the nonprofit.

- *The board has difficulty recruiting members.* Who are the members of the
  nominating committee? Does the board have a nominating committee? Those individuals who were recruited but turned down board
  membership should be contacted on a confidential basis to provide
  feedback on the recruitment and interview process. If it appears that
  a serious problem exists in the process for recruiting board members, the board leadership might utilize a "secret shopper" technique.
  The board leadership might enlist the cooperation of a disinterested
  third party in posing as a prospect for the board. This individual
  could, on a confidential basis, provide an objective perspective and
  useful recommendations for making membership on your board more
  attractive.

Looking Deeper: Organizational Citizenship and the Board

Although there may be many reasons to explain or describe why nonprofit
board members display LYBATD syndrome, the fundamental element at
play is an inherent lack of understanding of board member obligations of

organizational citizenship. Scholars over the years have described organizational citizenship in terms of an "extra-role behavior that is not formally recognized or rewarded by the organization." Behaviors that are associated with an individual's sense of organizational citizenship include "*loyalty* which is an allegiance to the organization and its leaders, *obedience* which describes an acceptance of the need for rules and regulations, and *participation* which is the full and responsible involvement in organizational governance."[2] These behavioral descriptions closely parallel the three legal standards of care, loyalty, and obedience that are required of all board members in their deliberations.

The paradigm of organizational citizenship is an essential expectation of governance within any organization. Board members and senior managers are expected to set the tone for ethical behavior as well as model the behavior. A report by the Committee of Sponsoring Organizations of the Treadway Commission in 1992 on the sources of corporate fraud emphasized that management must ensure that effective internal control needs to filter throughout the organization.[3] The COSO report and the work of other scholars conclude that the "tone at the top" contributes to the attitudes and subsequent behavior of everyone in the organization.[4]

CRAFTING INTERVENTION STRATEGIES FOR THE SYNDROME

Organizational Citizenship Behavior, LYBATD Syndrome, and Board Dysfunction

Organizational citizenship describes the individual's sense of his or her role within the organization and those expectations that the individual sees as his or her obligation to the organization.[5] These expectations are cultivated by those behavioral models that are passed along to members of the organization. The individual's sense of his or her organizational citizenship obligations can come in the form of small gestures, such as making another pot of coffee if he has poured the last cup or emptying her trash. More significant demonstrations of organizational citizenship include upholding high ethical standards and ensuring that all materials produced for the organization are accurate, well crafted, and consistent with the purpose of their design.

Board dysfunction, therefore, is not simply the result of one issue or even one person. Generally, board dysfunction reflects a synergy of factors relating to a basic lack of understanding about one's organizational citizenship and governance obligations. Board members have not been briefed regarding the legal standards of care, loyalty, and obedience. Because their fiduciary obligations are not clear to them, they do not understand what "governance" means in terms of role and deliverables. This is evidenced in board members not understanding why they need to prepare for board meetings prior to the meeting. When board members come to meetings unprepared to engage in meaningful discussion or decision making, they rely on passive acceptance of staff reports and are reluctant to exercise any critical thinking skills.

If the nonprofit's organizational culture and customs suppress board participation, it is often because board members do not see this behavior as spurning their legal responsibilities, especially those relating to fiduciary obligations. This is particularly problematic when board members are recruited for their social status and financial resources. This type of "means testing" as a prerequisite for board membership sometimes gives members a sense of entitlement. These board members feel that as long as they make significant financial contributions, they are exempt from any other board obligations.

Nonprofit management sometimes intentionally recruits passive individuals to establish a "window-dressing" board that is expected to rubber stamp management decisions. The board does not have solid leadership that provides a substantive orientation or articulates a performance agenda. This type of dysfunction emerges from management expectations that board members will do as they are instructed. The board never fully understands its governance role, nor does it understand that in today's environment, it can be held criminally liable for the nonprofit executive's actions.

Impact of LYBATD Syndrome on the Board's Performance

Boards experiencing LYBATD syndrome often have difficulty in accomplishing goals and objectives—if these have even been established. The board seems to go in circles of endless reports and meetings. LYBATD syndrome is evident in these types of problems:

- *Inability to fulfill governance role and expectations.* The board's lack of understanding about its obligations tends to be passed on to new members, which further perpetuates the syndrome. If a new board member objects or attempts to interject reality, the person often is subjected to negative feedback, which either extinguishes the behavior or causes the person to resign from the board.

- *Inability to attract competent board members.* Prospective board members who are educated on their legal and ethical obligations are unlikely to find LYBATD syndrome boards as attractive opportunities for service.

- *Inability to deal effectively with nonprofit management and provide direction to the organization.* The board in all probability does not have a shared vision of its role or governance expectations, which limits its ability to supervise the board's employee, the executive director, effectively.

- *Inability to understand and interpret the financial statements.* Boards suffering from LYBATD syndrome are not likely to have members who are financially literate. Financial literacy is essential in interpreting financial statements and identifying trends in the nonprofit's financial profile.

- *Decision-making ability.* LYBATD impedes the board's decision-making ability. Boards, are expected to engage in appropriate due diligence as they consider the decisions at hand based on reasonable consideration and rational discussion. Boards experiencing LYBATD often defer decision-making endlessly or employ arbitrary methods such as having the executive committee make the decisions and simply present the results to the rest of the board.

- *Inability to fundraise and represent the nonprofit in the community.* Boards experiencing LYBATD are less effective in their fundraising efforts because members are not fully engaged in their governance roles. Board members who are full participants in the governance of the nonprofit understand the goals and objectives of the organization's fundraising strategy and can convey it effectively to the community.

- *Inability to engage in strategic planning, business continuity planning, and risk management planning.* Boards experiencing LYBATD rarely have enough members present or interested or committed to engaging in planning of this nature. In LYBATD boards, members see their role as superficial and are quick to delegate important planning to the nonprofit's staff.

- *Inability to attract and retain competent staff and management.* Today's non-profit management and staff often have a private-sector background. Their experience and skills were honed in a working paradigm that emphasized bottom-line accountability and solid operational processes. To attract and retain these talented staff and management, the non-profit needs to have a board that will inspire confidence.

The Competent Board: Techniques for Eradicating LYBATD Syndrome

LYBATD syndrome is an outgrowth of either low or nonexistent expectations of board member performance and accountability. The ways in which board members are selected, screened, and introduced to the non-profit's board norms can eradicate LYBATD syndrome.

Board Member Selection: Recruitment, Screening, and Orientation

The current members of your nonprofit board may have been recruited from many sources—friends, relatives, donor database or nonprofit clearinghouses. Some of the members of the board have experience and credentials that are appropriate to the nonprofit, but others may be over their heads in terms of understanding their role and what is expected of them. SOX best practices presumes that all members of the board are qualified to serve, that is, competent to serve in a governance role, and possess an understanding of what is expected of them as well as a skill set that serves to accomplish expected performance.

Board members should be recruited based on those specific areas of expertise, diversity, or background that the board's leadership and nominating committee have identified as significant to the nonprofit. Under no circumstances should more than one member of a family be seated on the board, nor should a family member of any staff member be seated on the board. Similarly, vendors and consultants to the nonprofit should be disqualified for board membership. Those individuals who are seated on the board should also agree to sign a conflict of interest statement on an annual basis and should understand that they are required to disclose immediately any circumstances that could be considered a conflict of interest. In today's environment, even the appearance of a conflict of interest is unacceptable.

Board Orientation   How do board members learn about what is expected of them? LYBATD syndrome thrives when board members are unsure of what is expected of them or when a board operates in an environment that discourages questions and interaction. One of the best ways to offer a comprehensive introduction to board service and expectations is through an orientation and subsequent in-service training sessions. The orientation for new members should be crafted to address the important issues and articulate board performance expectations. The orientation is also the occasion for candid discussion of what is expected in terms of critical thinking, professional behavior, ethical standards, and current expectations of board accountability. Chapter 7 examines the structure and presentation of a board orientation.

Term Limits   When a board member joins the board, he or she should know the length of the appointment and the rules for reappointment to the board. These rules, however, are useless unless enforced. If your board does not have term limits, it is essential that these be instituted immediately—regardless of the outcry. Responsible board members will have no objection to the enforcement of term limits. Those who protest could be offered a seat on an advisory board. Note, however, that the well-being of your nonprofit is far more important than yielding to manipulative behavior.

Size of the Board and Board Composition   Depending on the size of the nonprofit, the ideal board size is somewhere between 7 and 16 members. Boards smaller than 7 can become deadlocked, and those larger than 16 can become unwieldy or experience a chilling effect on discussion and dissent, and possibly the emergence of a "ruling elite," which generally takes the form of the executive committee.

The board should establish procedures to ensure that new members are recruited, trained, and understand their roles and obligations including term limits. Boards should ensure that the size of the board is appropriate to the size and needs of the organization.

Performance Evaluation   Boards should also endeavor to evaluate their own performance as a governance entity and the performance of their individual members. These performance standards should include attendance at meetings, committee work, fundraising, preparation for discussion, participation in strategic planning, and other activities. Performance evaluations for all board members should be based on agreed-on performance objectives and take place on an annual basis.

Leveraging the Committee System to Cure LYBATD Syndrome
The board needs to develop an effective committee system or upgrade the current committee system to address SOX requirements and best practices. The committees will be expected to craft agendas that describe deliverables and their corresponding timelines. Members of the committee need to have job descriptions, performance objectives, and written behavioral norms. Upgrading committee performance begins with ensuring that competent, motivated people are seated as committee chairs. This does *not* mean that the chairs are all-powerful, like Wendell of the Spinnaker Society, but it does mean that the chairs are supportive of the executive committee's efforts to improve board performance and compliance with SOX and relevant state legislation.

Committees can be as small as 3 people or much larger, although committees of greater than 15 people can be cumbersome. Committees need not be populated exclusively from the board. Inviting prospective board members whose credentials are consistent with the committee focus to serve on a committee for a year or two can be useful to both the prospective member and the board. The individual can see how the board operates, and the board has the opportunity to see the individual in action.

Here are examples of the types of committees that are essential in implementing SOX requirements and best practices:

- *Executive.* The executive committee generally consists of the board chair, vice-chair, secretary, treasurer, and senior management team of the nonprofit. This committee is charged with the day-to-day governance of the organization, decision making at the executive level, and crisis management. This committee may negotiate the executive director's compensation package as well as the compensation packages of the other members of the senior management team. Important! The compensation packages for all executives must be approved by the entire board. The executive committee coordinates the implementation of SOX requirements and best practices and assigns the deliverables to the various committees and nonprofit senior management.

- *Finance.* The finance committee is responsible for reviewing the monthly financial reports, making decisions related to revenues and expenditures, and providing assertive oversight of all financial operations including purchase of insurance. Financial literacy for members of this committee is a must. This committee also ensures that the board and nonprofit carry adequate insurance. The nonprofit and the board need to be adequately protected. It is essential that the nonprofit purchase directors and officers liability, general liability, business interruption, automobile, property and casualty, and other important insurance coverage. The nonprofit's insurance professional is a key player on this team. He or she can provide advice on the types of policies that are right for your organization.

- *Audit.* Nonprofit boards need to have a separate audit committee that includes at least one board member who is a financial expert, but may *not* include members of the executive committee, management or staff, or members of the finance committee. The audit committee is responsible for selecting and retaining the auditor or person who will conduct a financial review for the nonprofit. The committee must ensure that auditors/reviewers are not also engaging in additional services, such as consulting, for the nonprofit. The committee is also responsible for ensuring that either the auditing firm is rotated every three to five years or that the lead auditor is rotated off the nonprofit's audit every three to five years. The audit committee facilitates a rigorous review of financial statements and transactions, acts as liaison between the board and the auditor/reviewer, and is also responsible for ensuring that all board members are financially literate. The committee has the power to present a required training program to ensure that all members of the board understand how to read and interpret financial reports. *A financially literate board is more likely to ask questions and insist on answers. Knowledge and empowerment are important weapons in eradicating LYBATD syndrome.*

- *Nominating and administrative.* The nominating committee is charged with recruiting and screening prospective board members and recommending a slate of new directors for the board's approval. This committee also ensures that the board's conflict-of-interest policy and code of ethics are in place and enforced. This committee needs to be the leader in ensuring that there is a strict prohibition against inside dealings, such as personal loans to any director or officer, and a human resources policy that prohibits lending money to the chief executive or chief financial officer, executive director, or other staff. This committee establishes policies that describe the types of behavioral expectations that relate to the roles of board members and members of senior management. No exceptions to these policies should *ever* be made.

- *Development and fundraising.* The development committee is charged with oversight into development and fundraising activities for the nonprofit. Often members of the development committee are expected to conduct development activities for the board itself. State laws, such as California's Nonprofit Integrity Act, require the board to provide active oversight into any and all contracts for fundraising vendors and activities.

Exhibit 4.3 summarizes the ways in which a competent board goes about implementing SOX requirements and best practices. To ensure that the requisite actions are taken, the board must be fully aware of the reality of the times and the expectations of accountability and transparency. Boards do not become competent instantaneously, but in today's environment, the transformation process needs to take place at an accelerated pace and with the understanding that nonprofits operate in a competitive environment. Failure to implement SOX requirements and best practices will put your nonprofit at a distinct competitive disadvantage. The nonprofit's external advisors, such as its banker, attorney, insurance professional, and information technology specialists, are essential in providing feedback on the board's action steps.

Keeping the board informed about current regulatory practices is a very effective defense against LYBATD syndrome. The proceedings of the Grassley Hearings, the report of the Independent Sector Panel on the Nonprofit Sector, and agencies such as the IRS provide materials to keep abreast of current developments in the legislative environment.

SUMMARY

SOX requirements and best practices actively address the factors that contribute to or are symptomatic of LYBATD syndrome. SOX requirements

EXHIBIT 4.3   SOX REQUIREMENTS AND
                BOARD RESPONSE

SOX Requirement/Best Practice	Board Action
Whistleblower protection	Ensure that there is a written policy and procedures for submitting and investigating a report.
Document preservation	Ensure that a written policy and procedures exist. Hold management and staff held accountable for compliance.
Audit committee	Ensure that audit committee is established and in place.
Certified financial statements	Ensure that board and management receive accurate and timely financial reports on a monthly basis.
Accuracy and timely submission of IRS 990 form	Actively oversee the preparation and submission of the 990. Ensure that the document is presented to the entire board with detailed explanations.
Higher level of board accountability	Upgrade and adhere to written policies on board membership requirements, orientation content, and performance expectations.
Conflict-of-interest policy and code of ethics	Ensures that all board members and senior management submit conflict-of-interest letters annually. Ensure that there is a written code of ethics for board and senior management alike.
Transparency at all levels of the organization	Ensure that there are written protocols for the reimbursement of travel claims and other reimbursable expenses that are strictly enforced.
Internal controls for all departments	Require management to demonstrate that internal controls are in place and enforced.
Consistent adherence to new policies and enforcement	Board members and senior management are kept apprised of current developments in nonprofit management and legislation.

and best practices introduce an unprecedented level of accountability and transparency in the way that nonprofit boards govern. With these standards, nonprofit boards are expected to display the same accountability and transparency private-sector corporate boards do. SOX best practices introduce a new level of professionalism within the internal operations of nonprofit boards and new performance expectations regarding nonprofit management and staff. State legislatures are mirroring the federal government in raising the accountability standards of nonprofits. The California Nonprofit Integrity Act was touted as a "SOX clone for nonprofits."

A competent board recognizes and accepts that there are steep consequences for scandals. Public sector scrutiny, particularly from regulatory or legislative entities, can signal legal sanctions or possibly revocation of nonprofit status. Additionally, media scrutiny can be very unforgiving—particularly when correspondence from legislators is publicized or donors have expressed concern about the way in which funds were solicited, accounted for, or disbursed. What might the impact on your nonprofit's board and operations be if a member of Congress declared your board to be the "poster child for why review and reform are necessary"?[6]

ENDNOTES

1. Mark W. Everson, testimony before the U.S. Senate Finance Committee, Washington, DC, June 2004.
2. Holmes et al., 2002.
3. Ibid.
4. COSO, 1992
5. Holmes et al., 2002.
6. Grassley, 2005.

CHAPTER 5

Moving the Board Forward: Intervention Techniques

Charles Dickens's legendary miser, Ebenezer Scrooge, could be considered a poster child for entrenched thinking and behavior. It took four ghosts (including Jacob Marley) and a vision of his own grave to finally get through to him. In one particularly compelling scene, the Ghost of Christmas Present opened his coat to reveal two shivering children, a boy and a girl, huddled beneath. The ghost bellowed to Scrooge, "Behold these children. The boy is 'Ignorance' and the girl is 'Want.' Take heed of them both, but beware of this boy."[1]

In an interview the year before he died, renowned scholar Peter Drucker was asked about his prolific writing career. Drucker commented that he had ideas for books that would have been better than the ones he had written. He would have called one of the books that he really wanted to write *Managing Ignorance.*[2]

Baseball great and noted philosopher Yogi Berra once observed that "ignorance isn't what you don't know; it's what you know wrong."

Ignorance comes in many packages and in many flavors, from a board chair who snarls, "Sarbanes-Oxley has nothing to do with nonprofits. You don't know what you are talking about," to board members who have no idea what legal expectations are associated with governance, to board members who allow themselves to be browbeaten by the nonprofit's senior management. The unfortunate tradition of ignorance within a nonprofit board eventually entrenches itself within the board and organizational culture.

ORGANIZATIONAL CULTURE

Every group, whether it is a nonprofit, business, social organization, church, or social club, has an organizational culture. This "culture" provides the members of the group with a type of organizational shorthand—a description of the organization's values, standards, behavioral norms, and ways of solving problems, what their traditions are, and how they solve problems.

How Does Organizational Culture Impact the Workings of the Board?

Sometimes when you walk into a nonprofit, you can just "feel" what it must be like to work there. Something about the way that people talk, or dress, or act sends out signals. Other clues come from the way that the offices look—are they cluttered and disheveled, or neat but cold? Some offices exude "high-class" pretension, while others have a distinctly "anti-establishment" feel.

The same thing happens when a new board member walks in to a board meeting for the first time. Learning to understand a board is much like peeling an onion; there are layers upon layers. From deep within the board come the "rules"—written and unwritten—about how things are done, how problems are solved, what is valuable, and, more important, *who is valuable*. The first thing that any board member needs to learn about is the board's power structure.

Where is the power?

- Is it the founder of the organization (who may have since retired from work) still seated on the board?
- Is it the major donor who bought and keeps paying for a seat on the board?
- Is it the socialite who gives the board visibility in the *Society Hill Gazette*?
- Is it the executive committee, whose members are a board unto themselves in which all of the deliberations and decisions take place?

Finding the power source is just the beginning. Generally a person or group of people are tasked with "showing the ropes" to newcomers. This is not to be confused with a board orientation. Often the unwritten rules come under the rubrics of "how to get along around here." The unwritten rules exist because either everyone agrees with them or everyone feels compelled to behave in compliance with them. The idea that the "way things are done around here" is a *shared notion* is key to understanding board culture.

Edgar Schein, noted expert on organizational behavior, defined organizational culture as a system of shared basic assumptions that helps people within the organization to cope with external forces, solve problems, and pass along the learned methods for dealing with day-to-day business.[3]

Organizational culture is reflected in the way newcomers are selected to become a part of the institution, whether the newcomers are new staff, administrators, volunteers, or board members. Once the newcomers have accepted the "invitation" to join the board in whatever capacity, what they are told about the board and how they are shown the ropes of routine institutional life is a reflection of organizational culture. Some boards are very open about how decisions are made, how ideas can bubble up, and how grievances are settled. Other boards have a very hierarchical structure, and sending messages upward requires elaborate protocols.

Probably the most powerful illustration of how an organization's "culture" works is in the types of behaviors that are either rewarded or have no consequences imposed. Even more important, what types of behaviors are either punished or extinguished? The terms "reward" and "punishment" here are not to be taken as entirely positive or negative. Some behaviors are discontinued—extinguished—because insufficient positive reinforcement has been extended. Consider the case of a board member who worked long into the night to review materials for the next evening's board meeting. If the board meeting's agenda is yet again ignored and the issues addressed in the materials are not discussed, how likely is it that the board member will devote this level of attention to future materials? Whether a behavior is repeated is often contingent on the degree of positive or negative reinforcement applied in immediate response to the behavior.

Behavior can be either reinforced or extinguished based on an organization's cultural environment, values, beliefs, and applicable resources. Every organization has a unique and irreplaceable "culture" that reflects a distinctive interaction of people within the organizational environment. In other words, the interaction serves to perpetuate the behavioral and cognitive norms that are part of the organization's culture while punishing or extinguishing behaviors and articulated (i.e., spoken out loud) values that are perceived as contrary to the established norms. What are the established norms in your board? What are board members criticized for saying or doing? In the story about the Spinnaker Society, the board member who questioned what he saw as a clear conflict of interest situation was reprimanded by the board chair for failing to accord the level of deference that the board chair felt the treasurer deserved.

Working to improve your board's organizational culture is an integral part of keeping your board operating as a highly productive governance entity. Improving the board's productivity means that the organizational culture needs to be changed to adopt new and better methods of governance and accountability. The board's overarching values, which are found in the mission statement, are a good place to start. It is essential that all of the board members become early adopters of SOX best practices.

Clues to Interpreting a Board's Culture

Organizational culture is not something that you can put in a container or under a microscope. However, there are important clues within every board to help the observer make sense of the current organizational culture.

Conversations   How do people within the board speak to each other? This point does not refer to what language is spoken. Rather, this element of board's culture centers on the manner and content of what is spoken. Do conversations take place in the open or in exclusive groups of the power elite? Are certain things kept secret from other board members? For example, does everyone on the board know how the details of the executive director's compensation package?

The member of a small nonprofit board confronted the board chair about why details of the executive director's compensation package were not shared with the rest of the board. The board chair declared, "The executive committee decides these things. It's none of the rest of the board's business." Fortunately for this board chair, her nonprofit is probably too small to hit Senator Grassley's radar screen.

Traditions and Ceremonies   Is the annual board picnic a "you are invited and will attend" event? What other special events are celebrated? Why are these or other events or gatherings significant within the board? Other traditions and ceremonies can include a volunteer awards ceremony or an award presentation named after a major donor. The board's culture can be observed in how these events are run and what the expectations are of the event and of the participants. How frequent are these events? If they occur on a regular basis, how much anticipation can be felt?

Behavioral Norms   Every board has behavioral norms—how members are expected to behave, to dress, to present themselves in terms of personal grooming, and to treat others. When a board member enters the nonprofit's offices, how is that person received? Behavioral norms also include attendance requirements, committee assignments, and even the level of financial gifts that mark the board member's generosity toward the nonprofit.

Rules of the Game   These are implicit rules for getting along as a board member. Sometimes the rules directly relate to navigating the dangerous shoals of intraboard politics or, even more perilous, navigating the politics that link the board and the senior management. The navigation charts for these waters are unwritten but very powerful in the consequences imposed for those who either ignore or unwittingly break the rules.

What are the rules for board member productivity? Sometimes board members are recruited specifically because they bring a needed skill set to the nonprofit. Other times individuals are recruited to sit on a board because an executive director needs their skills but is unwilling or unable to pay the market rate. A board seat often is an effective but disingenuous way to persuade a professional to provide services on a pro bono basis.

Beliefs and Values   The board's values are often embodied in the mission statement. However, other values and beliefs are entrenched within the organization but do not appear in the mission statement. Sometimes these beliefs and values parallel or support the mission, such as generosity, and concern for the community at large. Yet other beliefs and values can come into play within a board, such as not having to play by the rules because we are a nonprofit, or because we serve poor people, or because we serve rich people, or just because!

Policies and Protocols that Guide How a Board Conducts Operations
The way in which a board presents itself to major donors, funders, and the community can present clues as to what is or is not happening within the board. Although some boards take great pains to cover illegal behavior, they are by far the exception. Most boards are transparent about who they are and what they do. It is how this information is presented that holds the clue to the nonprofit's overall culture.

Problem-Solving   How does the board go about solving problems? Are there committees, ad hoc groups, just the executive director and the management team? What does the board consider a problem?

Strategic Planning   How does the board integrate mission and strategy, including goal setting? How does the board go about obtaining a consensus on the vision and direction of the organization? Do strategic goals emerge from the mission and its core values?

Goals   The way in which a strategic plan is developed is one clue about the board's culture. A far more revealing element is the way in which an evaluation strategy is implemented that measures the accountability, rewards, labor, and resources to achieve the goals in the strategic plan.

Intervention Strategies   How does the board come to the conclusion that it must take steps to change direction? Is the conclusion based on unmet goals, or a change in the external environment, or if internal processes are not meeting organizational needs? How long does it take for the board to realize that something dramatic must happen? For some boards, their reluctance to admit that there is a problem is an enormous barrier to progress.

The organization's culture is the synergy of these elements, although deciphering organizational culture can become a very complex process. Being open to hearing and seeing the clues is important, as these are the conduits to introducing change. Now more than ever, it is important to look closely at your board and its organizational culture. SOX best practices can be adopted only if the board is ready to implement and incorporate these practices in a new culture of compliance.

Impact of Nonprofit Dysfunction on the Board

Understanding the nonprofit's organizational culture is helpful in identifying its dysfunctional attributes and how these affect board functioning. Because organizational culture is intangible, observers need to look closely at the behavioral clues, the beliefs expressed, the stories told, and the way in which problems are solved. Each nonprofit is a unique entity because each is populated with unique individuals. Like any other organization, nonprofits have their own ways of doing things. Dysfunction within a nonprofit can be insidious, or it can be very obvious. Sometimes dysfunction is evidenced by the fact that nothing ever gets done. Other nonprofits mask their dysfunction with an aura of busyness. Yet others have highly dysfunctional boards, or management teams, or rank and file. Each of these groups can imprint its mark or malignancy on the nonprofit. Sometimes an autocratic leader, often the founder of the organization, can be the source—even a continuing source of dysfunction after he or she is fired. In one instance, a nonprofit's board terminated the highly dysfunctional founder of the organization but allowed the individual to remain on the board! Why? Most board members thought this person would be helpful in fundraising! Such ill-advised decisions are not the stuff of fiction—they happen every day.

Clues to Observing Dysfunction

Most of the time dysfunction is not something that can be readily identified. As you observe the goings-on in a nonprofit, be aware of clues that indicate problems and the spillover effect that the problems have on the board.

Attitudes and Beliefs   A dysfunctional belief system that perpetuates institutional ignorance is often at the root of organizational dysfunction. How often have you heard people on a nonprofit board say:

- We're poor, grassroots, small, not part of the "establishment," out in the boonies . . . [fill in the blank]. The litany of woes goes on forever.
- No one would investigate us, sue us, or [fill in the action].
- We're a nonprofit—we don't have to do all of the things that corporations are expected to do.

- We work too long and hard as it is. We're not going to do more work.
- Our staff isn't paid very well. I can't be expected to require high performance from them.
- She's a board member. She gives us her time and money—we can't ask her to actually *do* anything!
- I'm the boss here. I started this nonprofit and we'll do it my way. I know these clients better than anyone.
- That never works. We've tried it before.
- Senator Grassley really doesn't understand how nonprofits operate.

Although the nonprofit's values are often embodied in the mission statement, not all of the values appear there. Other values and beliefs that are entrenched within the organization but do not appear in the mission statement are often articulated through comments such as the ones just listed. Sometimes these beliefs and values parallel or support the mission, such as generosity and concern for the community at large. Other nonproductive beliefs and values, however, can come into play within a nonprofit. The sense of entitlement, specialness, or out-and-out adolescent rebellion on the part of people who are chronologically adults can have spectacular effects—on others and on the nonprofit.

What are the spillover effects on board functioning? If board members are immersed in the woe-is-us mentality of many nonprofits, they will be less inclined to employ rational and critical thinking to board deliberations. Low-functioning boards will find it very difficult to discern the value that implementing SOX requirements and best practices would bring to their nonprofit's overall operations. Equally important, they will be discouraged from asking the difficult questions, presenting alternatives, and adopting best practices. Many nonprofit executives actively promote the them versus us mind-set of nonprofit "victims" and encourage their boards to do the same. Regrettably, even in nonprofit trade publications, opinion pieces exhort nonprofits to resist attempts to implement best practices for fear that they will lose their unique grassroots quality. Now *that is "humbug"!*

Performance and Productivity   Dysfunction within the organization can also be detected in the quality and quantity of output. How productive are staff members? Are reports and other deliverables produced on time? Are deadlines routinely missed? Documents that are produced in a haphazard and unprofessional manner do not inspire confidence in the nonprofit. More important, unprofessionally presented materials suggest that the content could easily be inaccurate, misleading, or simply wrong. In some instances, such as an IRS Form 990, a sloppy submission could garner unwanted scrutiny and possibly an audit.

Performance issues relate to interpersonal interactions as well as to document preparation. How are clients and/or visitors treated when they enter the nonprofit? Have clients or visitors complained that they were either ignored or treated in a callous manner? These types of complaints are not nuisance issues; they must be taken seriously.

What are the spillover effects on board functioning? Boards of marginally productive nonprofits are probably used to hearing a litany of excuses as to why documents, reports, or other materials are not prepared in a timely fashion or in a professional manner. The bottom line, however, is that such boards are rarely, if ever, provided with substantive enough materials to make effective decisions or judgments.

Board members of these organizations are also likely to find that any number of public or private complaints about the quality of service, programmatic offerings, or differential treatment. As complaints mount, board members might find it more difficult to raise money for the nonprofit.

Organizational Dysfunction and the Lack of Internal Controls   Many nonprofit executives and board members believe that the concept of internal controls applies exclusively to finance and financial operations. Internal controls are, in fact, necessary for human resources, information technology, operations, crisis communication, governance, and administration. The absence of internal controls is evidence not only of sloppy technique but also of a culture that does not have standards or accountability. Not surprisingly, such a culture is likely to be dysfunctional, if for no other reason than because there is a lack of accountability.

What are the spillover effects on board functioning? Nonprofits that lack essential internal controls often have boards that do not understand the necessity of these controls, nor do they understand the risk that they are taking in failing to demand that controls be put into place. The proliferation of nonprofits that believe that having internal controls demonstrates a "sellout" to the establishment served as the catalyst for regulatory attention. Congress and state legislatures are under pressure from constituents who do not find "having a heart" sufficient in terms of nonprofit internal controls. It is hoped that the boards in these nonprofits have directors and officers insurance; they will need it.

Organizational Dysfunction and Information Technology The way in which technology is used, misused, or ignored can signal dysfunction within a nonprofit. One of the most common examples of dysfunction is the failure to stay current and to recognize that technology is an integral part of the internal control infrastructure. Sadly, many nonprofits fail to understand the degree to which they depend on technology. It is not just computers! The term "technology" relates to other important operational tools, such as software, hardware, laptops and notebooks, personal digital assistants (PDAs), cell phones, voice mail, e-mail, and Internet access. Failure to manage this array of technology adequately can indicate not only organizational dysfunction but also a serious risk to the nonprofit in the form of hackers; theft of confidential data; identity theft; potential for harassment of staff, donors, or others; and other liability scenarios.

The current legislative environment presumes a level of competence in the use and application of appropriate technology as an integral tool in internal controls. Current expectations are that all nonprofits understand how to use and manage the types of technology that are appropriate to their organizations. Because technology reaches across all sectors of a nonprofit, dysfunction within this operational component can have far-reaching effects.

What are the spillover effects on board functioning? In today's world of technology, board members need to have access to the nonprofit's e-mail, Web site, and intranet. The more highly developed the nonprofit's technology infrastructure, the better equipped it would be to provide financials and other reports to the board electronically.

Board members should expect to be provided with accurate information on the design, features, and ownership of the nonprofit's technology, including who "owns" the nonprofit's Web site. The person or organization that "owns" the website possesses the intellectual rights to everything on the website. For example, the board of a small arts organization was surprised to learn that its Web site was really owned by the ubiquitous volunteer-administrator. A board member who found this volunteer's behavior disconcerting decided to check the Web site, www.whois.com, to see who owned it. Her instincts were correct—and the web hosting for the site had to be disrupted while the matter was settled. The board eventually had to pay the volunteer to relinquish the rights to the website.

Organizational Dysfunction and Development and Fundraising   The manner in which a nonprofit chooses to raise funds for its continuing operation has the potential to show a positive or negative image to the donors and community at large. Organizational dysfunction can be evident in the manner in which a fundraising campaign is structured and executed. The quality of "customer service" that donors or patrons receive is also indicative of how well the nonprofit is functioning.

The quality of the overall planning and execution of a fundraising campaign can indicate levels of dysfunction within the organization. One example that became a public relations soap opera was a West Coast zoo's naming contest for two grizzly bears. The contest was initially open to the public. Then the zoo decided to auction off the naming rights and "pay-off" those public entries with free tickets to the zoo. Then the zoo's management decided that the winners of the auction really did not get to name the bears. Fortunately the couple who won the auction had the sense to ask the zoo to open the naming contest to the public. The fiasco went full circle.

Donor privacy is particularly important in today's nonprofit business environment. If the nonprofit does not appear to care about donors privacy or is more interested in selling donor information to obtain additional revenue, these traits are red flags. Similarly, the degree of care that the nonprofit takes to ensure the security of donor records is an indicator of the level of organizational functioning. Limiting access to confidential donor records is essential to the preservation of donor privacy. Staff members need to be carefully screened and *authorized* to ensure that there is no inappropriate communication with donors.

What are the spillover effects on board functioning? Senator Grassley's letter to the acting board chair of American University, discussed in Chapter 1, was undoubtedly a "Maalox moment" for the university's development director. It should also have been a collective upheaval for the rest of the board. Can you imagine the effect on your nonprofit if Senator Grassley characterized your board as "the poster child for why review and reform are necessary"?

Dysfunction in the nonprofit's development and fundraising can have a serious effect not only on the board's credibility but also on its ability to raise funds and in-kind services for the nonprofit. The board may also experience a serious gap in the quality of reports and data related to fundraising or even be in violation of state law, such as California's Nonprofit Integrity Act.

Organizational Dysfunction and Public Trust   Public trust is one of the most important assets that a nonprofit has—and at the same time, it is one of the most elusive. Public trust is not something that can be shown to staff, clients, donors, or even members of the public. This fragile and subtle feature is the life breath of a nonprofit (or private-sector company). But once it is compromised, the organism is either damaged or dies. Nonprofits that experience scandals or other crises do not always return to normal operation. Those that do not have a crisis communication plan, that fail to be transparent, or seem to resent public inquiries about financial records are showing signs of dysfunction.

Does your nonprofit have a plan for dealing with a crisis? What if a key member of the staff dies, becomes disabled, or is under investigation? Do you have a spokesperson? Or would you sound like the interim executive director who commented to a reporter, "The time is not ripe to make any public statements"? The local newspaper had just broken the story of fiscal mismanagement at a nonprofit organization that, ironically, was in business to help nonprofits manage their organizations more efficiently. Five months after his haughty pronouncement, the executive director was forced again to deal with the media—this time to announce the organization's closure.

What are the spillover effects on board functioning? The board needs to consider the role that the nonprofit plays in the community and what the long-term effects of damage to the nonprofit's public image would be. If the board has not anticipated its actions in the event of a crisis or developed a crisis communication plan, the nonprofit's image and credibility could be seriously damaged.

Organizational Dysfunction and Legal Issues   Dysfunctional organizations often either have no understanding about the significance of legal issues or engage in games of denial to justify their ignorance. Legal issues can relate to required filings, such as IRS Form 990s, workers' compensation claims, complaints to regulatory agencies regarding harassment or hostile environment claims, or even failing to understand the connection between the quality of internal controls and legal obligations.

Legal documents, such as contracts, leases, filings with state and federal regulators, and licenses, need to be secured in an orderly fashion. Dysfunctional organizations often fail to have a coherent filing system that provides quick access to documents when needed.

Many dysfunctional organizations do not understand how and why complaints can escalate into litigation, nor do they understand the techniques that can be employed to deescalate a situation. A common reason for pursuing litigation is that the aggrieved party was ignored, the allegations dismissed as trivial, or the person was treated with disrespect. Boards and senior management can take the same ostrichlike stance because it would be "too much work" or "cost too much" to establish solid policies and procedures.

What are the spillover effects on board functioning? In today's legal environment, boards are considered to be the ultimate authority in any nonprofit. Legal problems including litigation can be traced back to the board's failure to act in the manner of the reasonably prudent person or its failure to heed its fiduciary responsibilities. The United Way of the National Capital Area and the James Beard Foundation were forced to replace their boards due to crises.

HOW TO JUMP-START THE BOARD TO A HIGHER LEVEL OF PRODUCTIVITY

Any type of board intervention can benefit from a jump-start. Here are some examples of how implementation of SOX requirements and best practices can jump-start your board toward a higher level of productivity.

- *Change the dynamics of the status quo.* Talk with your banker, your auditor, and your insurance professional. These advisors can provide you with information on new laws, regulations, and industry standards that can serve as a catalyst for change. Ask them to make a presentation to the board on the SOX requirements and best practices.

They can utilize their professional position and role as "experts" to candidly describe the very unpleasant consequences that the board and the nonprofit will experience if these requirements and best practices are not implemented immediately. These messengers are respected professionals who have all of the information at hand.

- *Neutralize the influence of difficult people on the board.* Recruit at least three to five top-notch board members in the next six months. These individuals should present the types of skill sets that are currently missing from the board. They should be fully aware that they have been recruited to assist you in the transformation of the board and should work closely with you and your associates to craft effective strategies and tactics to set the transformation in motion.

- *Introduce term limits or a plan to enforce current term limits.* Establish an advisory council and board emeritus group without voting power. Eliminate deadwood or dysfunctional board members by shifting them to the board emeritus group. Even if a longtime board member is still valuable and viable, the rules have to be applied consistently. Invite this individual to sit on another committee until he or she is eligible to rejoin the board.

- *Develop an agenda of "deliverables"* based on traditional expectations and SOX best practices to establish priority areas for immediate action. Establish a core group within the board to develop a strategy to achieve the deliverables. Institute performance expectations, such as attendance, financial support, funding, voting, and other behavioral norms. Make the visions, strategy, tactics, and objectives clear to everyone on the board, and assign components of the plan to every board member. Failure to perform means they are invited to join the emeritus group—immediately.

- *Institute a conflict-of-interest policy* that includes an educational component. The educational component defines conflicts of interest; how to disclose a conflict of interest; and how to address conflicts in an appropriate manner—policy, protocols, and annual conflict-of-interest statements.

- *Ensure that board meetings are run in a businesslike fashion.* Ensure there is a timed agenda, rules for discussion, and, if necessary, limited discussion time prior to taking a vote. Conversation is not permitted to run on and obstruct the business that is slated for that meeting.

- *Enroll board leaders and/or senior management in assertiveness training* to deal actively with dysfunctional board members, management, staff, volunteers, and/or other situations. The future of the nonprofit is at stake. The nonprofit's leaders need to feel empowered to bring the organization into compliance.

- *Establish an audit committee* whose role is to oversee the annual audit or financial review (for small nonprofits) and to upgrade the financial literacy of the board. Doing this can serve to change the dynamics of a dysfunctional board dramatically. The committee is expected to work in conjunction with the nonprofit's auditor or financial reviewer. The committee's findings are shared with the entire board. These findings are very helpful in identifying the more prominent areas of dysfunction. The financial professional who is conducting the audit or the review is in a position to make it clear that change has to be implemented immediately.

- *Ensure transparency* at all levels of management and in all transactions, including travel claims and reimbursements. There will be no punishment for whistleblower activities and no destruction of any documents during any investigation or litigation.

- *Adhere consistently to new policies and procedures and ensure enforcement.* A dysfunctional board will never fully recover unless everyone on the board knows that there are consequences for failing to stay in compliance with the changes.

An effective intervention strategy requires commitment by a majority of the board and/or executive committee, a vision of how the intervention will facilitate real and lasting change, and the ability to handle the ensuing conflict in a calm, unemotional fashion that emphases the board's commitment to being in compliance with the law.

Summary

In order to implement real and lasting change, the board needs to candidly examine how it does business. It needs to take the necessary steps to adopt

Sarbanes-Oxley requirements and best practices. The board needs to commit to utilizing current resources, such as professional advisors, to leverage new expectations of board performance as the framework for a brighter tomorrow.

ENDNOTES

1. Dickens, 1986 edition.
2. Feder, 2005.
3. Schein, 1992.

CHAPTER 6

Start at the Beginning

Assessing where your board is in terms of Sarbanes-Oxley compliance, adaptation of best practices, and purposeful board culture and performance is quite a challenge. Developing a "profile" of your board that identifies what is already in place and what needs to be either put in place or modified is an efficient way to determine your board's current status. This chapter features a questionnaire that will facilitate development of this profile.

QUESTIONNAIRE

The questionnaire is designed to help you and your board identify those areas that need priority attention, those areas are already in place and can be leveraged, and those areas that you might need to discuss with your nonprofit's professional advisors. These advisors include your banker, auditor, legal counsel, insurance professional, and information technology professional. They can help your board better understand how to bring your nonprofit into compliance and how to scale the "to do" list to better fit the size of your organization and board. For example, if your board is too small to have a committee structure, that is fine for now. Just concentrate on completing the tasks that would be the primary deliverables for each of the committees. As your nonprofit grows, the board can institute a committee system.

The Board and Its Composition

1. How are board members selected? What credentials, experience, or references are they expected to present? Does the nominating committee check references of board members?

2. What steps has the board taken to ensure that the board members are independent (i.e., not encumbered by personal relationships with other board members or senior management)?

3. What additional strategies might be put in place to identify and recruit individuals whose skill sets would enhance the board's collective capacity?

4. Does the board have term limits for its members?

5. How many consecutive terms are board members permitted to serve? Are the term limits enforced?

6. Are board members required to attend board orientations? Do the orientations contain substantive information that would facilitate understanding of the board member's role, legal requirements, and performance objectives?

7. Are board members briefed on the nonprofit's mission and how that mission is affected by board decisions?

8. Are board members briefed on how their decision making and their fiduciary obligations impact the nonprofit's mission?

9. Are board members briefed on the correlation between the quality of their performance and the nonprofit's mission?

10. Do board members receive performance evaluations?

11. Does the board have a nominating/governance committee? Some of the tasks that come under this committee's purview are nominating qualified candidates to stand for election to the board and compliance with ethical standards.

The Board and Its Governance Obligations

1. Does the board spend sufficient time and attention to provide the appropriate level of governance and oversight?

2. What areas of the nonprofit operations and/or management need additional attention?

3. Does the board have a conflict-of-interest policy?

4. Are board members required to disclose real or possible conflicts of interest on an annual basis?

5. Does the board have specific protocols to handle conflicts of interest as they occur?

6. Is the policy enforced in terms of prohibition of self-dealing and loans to directors or senior management?

7. Does the board have a code of ethics?

8. Does the board communicate to personnel at all levels of the non-profit a strong, ethical tone at the top, set by the board, the chief executive officer, and other senior management, establishing a culture of legal compliance and integrity?

9. Has the board assigned to the chief executive officer or other officer the specific task of serving as compliance officer?

10. Are board members furnished with financial statements and other materials well in advance of board meetings?

11. Are board members able to read and interpret these financial statements? How does the board leadership determine if members are able to understand the financial statements?

12. Are board meetings scheduled and conducted on a regular basis?

13. Are board members required to attend a specific number of meetings?

14. Prior to the meeting, do board members receive the meeting agenda and other materials needed for discussion and decision making?

15. Does the entire board meet regularly in executive session (i.e., without management and staff)?

16. Are minutes kept for each meeting and included as part of the packet for the next board meeting?

17. Do board members come to the meetings prepared to discuss the issues on the agenda?

18. Is there a specific decision-making process: that is, specific length of time for discussion followed by a vote?

19. If a topic needs to be deferred for a vote at a later date, are there specific steps and/or information that will be gathered so the board can take a vote when the topic is revisited?

20. Does the board have a system of committees that address important functional areas?

Committee Structure

Executive Committee

1. How often does the executive committee meet?

2. Does the executive committee make the majority of the board decisions, or are the decisions deliberated at full board level?

3. Does the executive committee negotiate the compensation packages of the executive director and the senior management team?

4. How does the executive committee share the details of these packages with the rest of the board before a vote is taken?

5. Does the executive committee conduct unannounced audits of the nonprofit's travel claims and expense reimbursements?

Finance Committee

1. How often does the finance committee meet?

2. How are financial reports prepared: in what format and how often?

3. Does the finance committee conduct an annual review of the nonprofit's insurance portfolio?

4. Has the finance committee reviewed the internal controls for the financial management function?

Audit Committee

1. Does the board have an audit committee or a financial review committee that is independent of the board's executive committee and the nonprofit's senior management?

2. Does the auditor provide services to the board or the nonprofit in addition to the audit?

3. How long has the auditor been associated with the nonprofit? If it is over five years, the auditor needs to rotate off the account and another auditor from his or her firm needs to conduct the audit.

4. Does the nonprofit use the auditing firm for nonauditing services? Doing so diminishes the independence of the auditor and presents a potential conflict of interest.

5. Does the board conduct an annual external financial audit or a financial review?

6. Does the audit committee include at least one "financial expert," which could be an individual who is external to the board?

7. Does the board ensure that all members on the audit committee do not present conflicts of interest and are not receiving any compensation for their service on the committee? (This includes any outside experts who have been recruited to serve on the committee.)

8. Has the board ensured that the audit committee selects the auditing company and works with the auditor to facilitate the completion of the audit?

9. Does the audit committee understand its role in reviewing the audit and serving as liaison to the full board to approve audit results?

10. Has the board ensured that the audit committee is tasked with providing financial literacy training to all board members?

11. Does the board demand adequate information from staff to provide data that is necessary and sufficient on financial issues?

12. Use auditors proactively identify problem areas in financial reporting systems and internal controls?

13. Do auditors distribute monthly benchmark statements to audit committee and staff?

14. Do auditors disclose all financial information to employees, funders, and the general public?

Personnel and Compensation Committee

1. Does the committee ensure that all appropriate documentation on executive contracts, compensation packages, and expense reimbursements is in order and presented to the full board?

2. Are compensation policies for all management and staff in line with industry standards? In other words, has the board engaged in due

diligence to ensure that compensation packages for all management and staff are consistent with nonprofit industry standards?

3. Does the committee make known to the full board the compensation packages for senior management?

4. Are executive compensation packages taken before the full board for a vote?

5. Has the committee established protocols for reimbursement of expenses, including travel claims? Are these protocols enforced for all paid staff and volunteers, including executives?

6. Has the committee conducted random, unannounced audits or reviews of reimbursements to ensure that documentation is in place and that the nature of the expense is legitimate?

7. Has the board implemented a whistleblower protection policy that is utilized throughout the nonprofit? Is there a mechanism to make such reports without fear of retaliation? Is there a mechanism for objectively investigating such reports and providing the individual making the report with the findings of the investigation?

8. Does the board routinely receive reports on the nature of the reports and the findings of the investigations?

9. Does the committee have procedures in place for the administration of contracts, including bidding protocols, selection of contractors, and payment of services and preparation of 1099 documents?

10. Are there protocols in place to permit no-bid contracts? If so, what are the safeguards against self-dealing or conflicts of interest?

11. Has the board mandated that the nonprofit develop a document preservation policy which includes a prohibition against destruction of documents during an investigation? Has the document preservation system been tested to ensure that documents are stored and archived appropriately?

    1. Have the chief executive officer and chief financial officer signed off on all financial statements (either formally or in practice), including Form 990 tax returns, to ensure they are accurate, complete, and filed on time?

    2. Has the board reviewed and approved financial statements and Form 990 tax returns for completeness and accuracy?

12. Has the board appointed a senior manager as compliance officer to ensure that all staff and management engage in ethical conduct and that the nonprofit is in compliance with all relevant laws and regulations?

13. Are IRS 990 forms filed on an annual basis? Are these filings accurate, complete, and prepared according to the updated requirements of the IRS?

14. Are board members furnished with financial statements and other materials well in advance of the board meetings?

Development and Fundraising Committee

1. Has the committee reviewed the internal controls of the development division of the nonprofit?

2. Are the operations of the development division of the nonprofit in compliance with the laws of the state in which the nonprofit is located and with the laws of the states in which it conducts business?

3. How are cash and receipts processed from fundraisers?

4. How are volunteers briefed prior to a fundraising event? Is there a discussion about how staff and volunteers are the public face of the nonprofit? Are behavioral standards presented and enforced?

5. Does the development committee audit the financial reports for each fundraiser to ensure that all revenue is recorded and that expenses corresponding to the generation of revenue are documented?

The Board and Its Oversight Role

How does the board provide oversight in areas of:

1. Financial operations
2. Internal controls
3. Compliance with federal, state, and local laws and regulations
4. Awarding of contracts: Is there a mechanism for ensuring that individuals who are awarded contracts are eligible to bid on and accept the engagement?
5. Policies and procedures for the processing of expense reimbursements, travel claims, and other payments to staff and management outside of their compensation packages

6. Pension plans and employee investment plans

7. Administration of public sector grants and contracts

8. Reviewing detailed *monthly* financial statements on a timely basis

9. Are there random checks of internal controls, such as protocols for reimbursement of travel claims and credit card charges.?

10. How does the board ensure that an ethics-related norm is included in employee qualification standards and in employees' annual performance reviews?

11. Are there human resources policies in place that stipulate segregation of duties, particularly in task assignments in finance or development?

12. Are all employees and volunteers briefed on ethical conduct and what the nonprofit's expectations are in terms of carrying out assignments in an ethical manner?

UTILIZING THE DATA FROM THE QUESTIONNAIRE AS A PLATFORM FOR CHANGE

The ancient Chinese had a saying that "a journey of a thousand miles begins with a first step." Moving your board and nonprofit to adopt SOX requirements and best practices may seem like a thousand-mile journey, but the task can be easily segmented into doable components. Use the questionnaire to identify those areas that should be given priority as your board begins its work. The answers to the questions provide a thumbnail sketch of your board's current compliance status.

Begin by reviewing the board's role in governance and accountability. Is the board in charge of the nonprofit, or has the board become the rubber stamp of the executive director and senior management? If it is necessary to reclaim the board's authority, then that must be the first step. If the board does not understand, accept, and *insist* on its role as the ultimate authority in the nonprofit, the nonprofit will never be in compliance with Sarbanes-Oxley legislation or state laws, such as California's Nonprofit Integrity Act.

If your responses to the questionnaire indicated that your board does not have many of the organizational elements in place, that is a signal that your work must begin immediately. The initial step to compliance starts with scheduling board meetings at regular intervals. If your board has not been meeting regularly up to this point, you must begin to schedule—and conduct—meetings; prepare substantive agendas; take attendance; decide on deliverables for the next 30, 60, 90, and 120 days; and, above all, insist on real and lasting change. It is essential to garner board cooperation from the onset—and board commitment to participate actively in the work needed to make these changes. Those board members who are unwilling to participate should be thanked for their service and removed from the board *immediately*. The board's leaders need to send an unequivocal message to the other board members and to the nonprofit's management and staff.

DEVELOPING YOUR BOARD'S CURRENT PROFILE

The questionnaire has helped your board to identify what it has in place and what additional areas of development are needed. The findings will serve as a framework for determining the policies and procedures that your board already has in place so that your board can begin to develop blueprint for action. The profile needs to describe your current board in terms of:

- Number of members
- Current standing committees
- Board and committee leadership
- Skill sets represented on the board (i.e., finance, law, information technology, art, etc.)
- Policies and procedures in place (e.g., does the board have a conflict-of-interest policy, code of ethics, nomination and placement procedures, board orientation, etc.?)
- Governance activities, such as policy-making, oversight, and compliance. Provide descriptions of these activities and proof—reports or other documents—that the activities are in place.
- Compliance with Sarbanes-Oxley requirements and best practices. If some or all of the SOX best practices are in place, provide supporting evidence such as a written policy or a report that proves your board

has adopted the best practices. Nonprofit boards must show that they are in compliance in these areas:

- The board is the ultimate authority in the management and operation of the nonprofit. This means that the board is in charge—not the executive director, not the chief financial officer, and not the chief operating officer. The executive director is the board's employee, and his or her senior management team is expected to perform its duties as directed by the executive director and board.

- The nonprofit has a whistleblower protection policy; a means by which staff and volunteers can report suspected waste, fraud, and abuse; and a means by which the reports are investigated and findings disseminated.

- The nonprofit has a document preservation policy containing a prohibition against destroying documents while an investigation is taking place.

- The nonprofit properly prepares an annual IRS Form 990, which is submitted on time and is complete and accurate.

- Board members approve the compensation package(s) for senior management.

- Board members establish and enforce a code of ethics.

- They establish and enforce a conflict-of-interest policy.

- They establish an audit committee and ensure that the nonprofit has either an annual audit or financial review.

- They ensure that the auditor is independent and does not provide other services to the nonprofit, such as bookkeeping, financial software installation or customization, or tax preparation.

- They review, interpret, and question financial statements prepared by staff.

- They ensure that the nonprofit's internal controls are in place and are enforced.

BLUEPRINT FOR ACTION

Once you have compiled the board's profile, it will be easier to identify what needs to be done to bring the board into full compliance. Building a blueprint for action need not be complicated, and the blueprint should not be so cumbersome that it becomes a barrier rather than a road map! Here are three easy steps to building an blueprint—and by developing a profile, your board has already completed Step 1.

Step 1—What is Your Board's Current Compliance Status?

The board's profile provides a comprehensive assessment of the board's current compliance status. For the purpose of the blueprint, *summarize* the findings from the profile. Indicate what your board already as in place and what is needed to bring the board into compliance with SOX and in line with best practices In order to consider a practice or protocol officially "in place," it must be in writing and be readily available for staff, management and board members to use as a resource. Even if certain practices are understood to be in place, these must be committed to writing.

Step 2—Identify Compliance Requirements or Best Practices Desired

Review the list of requirements and best practices and identify those that your board needs to adopt or implement at a higher quality. As your board works on its blueprint, it is important to obtain input from your nonprofit's professional advisors. Speak with the nonprofit's banker, legal counsel, and insurance professional. If your nonprofit has a Web site, e-mail, and numerous databases and electronic files, your board needs to also consult with an information technology professional to ensure that precautions have been taken to safeguard the files, hardware, and software.

Step 3—Prioritize Next Steps in Terms of Desired Deliverables, Time, and Resources

Here your board needs to sequence the deliverables—what needs to be done. Decide what needs to be completed in 30 days, 60 days, 120 days, 6 months, and 1 year. Emphasize those results that bring the board and the nonprofit in compliance with SOX and any relevant state legislation, such as California's Nonprofit Integrity Act.

It is equally important to delegate responsibility and accountability to those individuals assigned with the specific tasks. The board leaders should take on very few tasks; instead, the tasks for bringing the board into compliance should be spread throughout the entire board. Those individuals who are unwilling or unable to participate should be thanked for their service and removed from the board immediately. Your board may want to establish an advisory council if this is a politically expedient way to shift the deadwood. However, it is essential that the entire board understands that the quality of their performance will determine whether they are permitted to remain on the board. Your nonprofit can no longer afford to accommodate slackers.

LEVERAGING THE BLUEPRINT: ESTABLISHING STRATEGIES FOR LASTING CHANGE

The blueprint will serve as a framework for instituting lasting change in your board and in your nonprofit. Chapter 7 describes the ways in which your board and nonprofit can establish a platinum standard in governance using the SOX requirements and best practices. The recommendations for these practices began with the Grassley White Paper but were also recognized by the Independent Sector's Panel on Nonprofits as important for helping nonprofits and their boards to upgrade performance and accountability. The Independent Sector convened a blue ribbon panel that examined the recommendations for change that emerged from the Grassley White Paper and testimony before the Senate Finance Committee in 2004. The recommendations from the final report indicate how governance standards have been raised.

Recommendations from the Independent Sector Final Report

The Independent Sector's *Report to Congress and the Nonprofit Sector on Governance, Transparency and Accountability* contains the following recommendations:

> The board of a charitable organization should, as recommended practice or in accordance with the laws of its state:
>
> - Review the Form 990 or 990-PF filed by its organization annually.
> - ·Undertake a full review of its organizational and governing instruments, key financial transactions, and compensation policies and practices at least once every five years.
> - Include individuals with some financial literacy in its membership.

- Incorporate into the organization's by-laws, articles, charter, or other appropriate governing documents a requirement that the full board must approve, annually and in advance, the compensation of the CEO.
- Adopt and enforce a conflict-of-interest policy consistent with the laws of its state and tailored to its specific organizational needs and characteristics.
- Establish policies and procedures that encourage individuals to come forward with credible information on illegal practices or violations of adopted policies of the organization. The policy should specify that the organization will protect the individual who makes such a report from retaliation.

The report goes on to include these recommendations for Congress and regulatory agencies:

- Educate, in partnership with the IRS and state oversight officials, charitable organizations about financial transactions that are potentially abusive tax shelters and the additional reporting requirements and risks such transactions may pose.
- Provide information and education to organizations on the roles and responsibilities of board members and the factors that boards should consider in evaluating the appropriate size and structure needed to ensure the most effective, responsible governance.
- Educate charitable organizations about the importance of the auditing function.
- Educate and encourage all charitable organizations, regardless of size, to adopt and enforce policies and procedures to address possible conflicts of interest and to facilitate reporting of suspected malfeasance and misconduct by organization managers.
- If there was any lingering doubt that the times have changed and nonprofit boards are being held to a higher standard, this report and the Grassley White Paper should remedy that outdated thinking.

Summary

Nonprofit boards can measure their current level of compliance and best practices by developing a profile based on the questionnaire included in this chapter. The intent is to facilitate a streamlined effort to identify those tasks that need to be undertaken to improve the quality of the board's governance and oversight.

Establishing a Platinum Standard for Governance

Harry was the executive director (ED) of a nonprofit that provided healthcare education. He was a hardworking individual whose board largely included major donors to the nonprofit. Many of the board members felt that their donor status entitled them to treat Harry as if he was their butler. After several years of this type of abuse, Harry let it be known that he wanted his hard work acknowledged with a pay raise. The board president, who was one of the more arrogant board members, began proceedings to fire Harry. In the meantime, Harry was hospitalized for quadruple bypass surgery. His subsequent convalescence was approximately six weeks. The board wanted to move ahead with Harry's termination despite the admonishment of one board member who advised the board that they were in violation of state laws and the Americans with Disabilities Act (ADA) because Harry was a member of at least two protected classes: age and disability. The board member insisted that a memo from her be placed in the minutes so that, in the event of any litigation, there would be evidence that the board was warned and that the board member who authored the memo would not be held individually liable. The board pressed on with their termination of Harry, and he filed a complaint with the state labor board. The proceeds of the legal settlement allowed Harry to purchase a lovely vacation home in the country.

This chapter presents present methods for improving the board's decision-making, fundraising, and governance quality, including how to leverage Sarbanes-Oxley to move your board as a governance entity from mediocre to stellar. Here are some examples of the types of results that your board would want to see:

- Recruit superior board members.

- Increase productivity and conduct more substantive board meetings.

- Improve fundraising results.

- Stipulate (and receive) better performance from the executive director and his or her staff.

- Save on overhead costs and create a higher level of organizational efficiency.

- Position the nonprofit to be more attractive to funders such as foundations and high-wealth individuals.

SOX Best Practices: Moving to a Platinum Operating Standard

Moving to a "platinum" operating standard represents a synergy of the nonprofit's values (i.e., mission), operational efficiency, and regulatory compliance. Nonprofits pride themselves on their commitment to fulfilling their mission—and some see that as the end of the story. That is a short-sighted approach in today's business environment. Yes, nonprofits do operate within a business environment—they compete for revenue in the form of funding and customers: clients and donors. The metaphor of the "invisible hand of competition" made famous by eighteenth-century economist Adam Smith affects nonprofits as well as private-sector corporations. The difference between nonprofits and their private-sector counterparts primarily appears to be in organizational mind-set. Corporations understand and accept that they operate within a highly competitive environment and that they are expected to conduct operations in a businesslike fashion. Some nonprofits have not realized this.

Many nonprofits often fail to understand that in order to compete, they must enter the competitive arena as fully established organizations. If the board employs restrictive mind-sets about the organization, such as the demeaning "mom and pop," "poverty," or "we're small," they do a disservice to a nonprofit's clients, donors, staff, and community. The time has come for many in the nonprofit world to compete for resources as fully mature, fully competent organizations, regardless of organizational size. To that end, this chapter discusses the steps that an organization must take to move from an ordinary standard to a platinum standard.

Often mission-driven and grassroots organizations tend to deemphasize organizational infrastructure while focusing on programs or fundraising. Some have even reached the point where fundraising is the most important venture, as the organization is living hand to mouth. Frequently the boards of these organizations consist of donors or members of the community who have been associated with the organizations for decades. One nonprofit, whose affiliation with a world-renowned charity should have resulted in sustained growth, stalled in its development because its board was populated with its founder's friends and board appointees hand-picked by the founder. The board president, who was the nonprofit's largest donor, felt entitled to keep the job for over 20 years. The chair of the finance committee was an employee of the nonprofit's financial institution, which created a conflict of interest, or at least the appearance of one. A new executive director, who had twenty-first-century ideas and stellar nonprofit management experience, was stymied at every turn by this board, which initially claimed to never have conflicts.

An even more spectacular example of a grassroots organization's sticky situation comes in the form of a financial scandal at a West Coast watchdog group. Published reports indicated that independent auditors determined that a half million dollars was unaccounted for primarily through "poor bookkeeping, administrative failure or theft. . . ." At the heart of the financial irregularities was the practice of making questionable loans to employees and board members, including the board treasurer. Virtually none of these loans were repaid. The newspaper account indicated that making loans of this type was a longtime practice. In defense of this loan practice, the ousted ED claimed, "In organizations that work with poverty, there is often the need to take these types of emergency measures." Using the spurious claim that his organization was "working with poverty," this former ED insinuated that a "poverty mentality" is justification for subverting donor funds.[1] *No, it is not!*

Loans to employees or board members can never be justified under any circumstances. There is never any justification for betraying the trust of the community to satisfy the monetary desires of board or staff. If your nonprofit is operating with a poverty mentality, the time has come to summon the courage to make a dramatic change before your organization's slipshod operations make the front page of your city's newspaper or become the lead story on the evening news.

WHAT ARE PLATINUM OPERATING STANDARDS?

Nonprofits that adopt a platinum operating standard recognize that regulatory legislation is not necessarily just an attempt by the public sector to intrude on their operation. Legislation such as the Sarbanes-Oxley Act is intended to introduce, admittedly by requirement, those practices that should have been in place all along. The employees, shareholders, and creditors of Enron, Arthur Andersen, WorldCom, and the United Way of the National Capital Area would be much happier and more solvent today if those organizations had embraced what we now call the SOX best practices. Nonprofits committed to moving their operations to a platinum standard recognize that in order to grow and thrive, they have to be the best that they can be. This means that all of their systems and internal controls have to be functional, seamless, in compliance with regulations and industry best practices. Yes, there is a nonprofit industry—just look at all of the conferences, books, journals and other products targeting the nonprofit world.

Here are some characteristics of nonprofit boards that have adopted platinum operating standards:

- *A more effective board whose members understand and adhere to their fiduciary obligations and recognize their responsibility in governing the nonprofit.* Board members are able to make decisions within the context of care, loyalty, and obedience. The board decisions and policies serve to move the nonprofit's management to implement SOX requirements and best practices fully.

- *Higher level of management and staff accountability.* The board is able to craft solid strategies for organizational effectiveness and provide management and staff with the guidance to upgrade internal controls and improve the level of transparency within the organization.

- *Effective protocols to ensure that the nonprofit remains in compliance with SOX and nonprofit "industry standards" and addresses future standards.* The board ensures that a protocol is in place to keep abreast of new legislative developments and new industry standards.

- *Better competitive positioning by making known that the nonprofit adheres to the SOX platinum standard in its operating practices.* The board and senior management work collaboratively to develop strategies for marketing that include leveraging compliance with SOX requirements and best practices.

- *Greater credibility and ability to recruit high-quality board members and to attract the favorable attention of major donors, foundations, and other funding sources.* The board and nonprofit's implementation of SOX requirements and best practices will make the nonprofit attractive to high-quality individuals who have excellent credentials and skill sets that will help to move the nonprofit forward. Adaptation of SOX requirements and best practices show that the nonprofit is committed to excellence in management and to ensuring that donor money is spent appropriately.

- *Financially literate boards.* Board members can read and understand financial statements. Financially literate board members can identify trends in the financial status of the nonprofit and ask the difficult questions when the nonprofit's financial health appears to be failing.

Board Role in Facilitating Platinum Operating Standards

The benefits of SOX requirements and best practices can be translated into higher performance through meaningful change in the nonprofit's culture and operations. The board gains nothing from permitting the nonprofit's management and staff to engage in minimal compliance with SOX. In order to achieve a higher level of performance, the board needs to work closely with the executive director, senior management, staff, and volunteers to introduce these change agents.

The board needs to take these steps to move to a platinum operating standard:

- *Recognize and accept that Congress, the IRS, regulators, state legislatures, and the courts* are now holding nonprofit boards ultimately accountable for the management and operations of the nonprofit.

- *Take the lead in communicating the deeper meaning of Sarbanes-Oxley legislation.* Donors, clients, and the public should have confidence that the nonprofit provides services in a transparent fashion in their community. Many nonprofits would prefer to whine about the unflinching provisions of this law and the expectations of its best practices. Introducing meaningful change requires a steadfast adherence to these requirements and best practices. The SOX requirements and best practices are protocols that every organization—private sector or nonprofit—should have been doing all along.

- *Establish the intention for change.* Central to setting a resolute tone is the expectation that governance and accountability will be taken to a higher level in your nonprofit. The board sets the tone by modeling the desired behavior. Implementing SOX requirements and best practices without fully expecting a higher level of efficiency and performance is a waste of everyone's time.

- *Every five years, conduct a full review* of the nonprofit's legal documentation to ensure completeness, the nonprofit's programming to ensure that the programs are consistent with the nonprofit's mission, and the financial statements to identify trends and patterns over that time frame. The review should also examine other documentation to identify trends, such as insurance claims, newspaper reports about the nonprofit, fundraising results, human resources complaints, and disciplinary action against individuals within the organization.

- *Every year, require senior management to present detailed reports of program and fundraising evaluations* and a complete description of the metrics used to evaluate programs and fundraising.

- *Every year, meet in executive session with the nonprofit's auditor and the audit committee.* No staff members should be permitted to attend this session. The auditor should be required to identify areas that he or she sees as potential problems or opportunities for fraud, or where real fraud is taking place. If the accountant gives the nonprofit a management letter, the issues cited in the letter should be rectified immediately and the improvements must be documented. Exhibit 7.1 is a worksheet for audit committees.

- *Commission the development of an organization-wide risk management plan and business continuity plan.* The plans should be reviewed and updated

EXHIBIT 7.1	AUDIT COMMITTEE WORKSHEET

Every nonprofit should have an audit committee, no matter how small the nonprofit or its board. The purpose of the committee is to provide oversight to the annual audit or, for small nonprofits, the annual review of financials.

Committee Composition
- One financial professional
- Two to four members of the board who are not also members of the finance committee

Committee Functions and Deliverables:

☐ Serve as a liaison between the auditor and the board.

☐ Ensure that the auditing firm is appropriate for a nonprofit audit (skill set and experience).

☐ Review the performance of the auditing firm.

☐ Ensure that the auditor provides auditing services only and no other services.

☐ Ensure that the auditing firm or partner is rotated every three to five years. If the auditing firm is large enough, then other partners or associates can rotate to provide auditing services to the nonprofit. In any event, members of the auditing firm should not be recruited to serve on the nonprofit's board or on the auditing committee.

☐ Ensure that the nonprofit's auditor has no financial or business connections to individual board members.

☐ Meet with the auditor to review the audit and make recommendations regarding board approval, or provide recommendations for modifications. The committee makes these recommendations to the full board, which ideally meets with the auditor to discuss the audit.

☐ Ensure that if the audit produces a management letter, the issues outlined in the letter are remedied immediately.

---

on an annual basis. Brief outlines of these plans can be found in Appendix C.

- *Talk openly about fraud.* One of the most difficult topics for boards to address or even talk about is fraud. No one likes to believe that people in their organization (particularly nonprofits) would ever steal or use resources in inappropriate ways. If you believe that there is no chance of fraud in your nonprofit please, stop reading this chapter and go to Appendix A, which is the full text of Senator Grassley's letter to American University's acting board chair, and then come back to this paragraph. *The board must candidly and assertively address the issue of fraud before internal controls can be strengthened and before the rest of the organization can be expected to understand why "business as usual" is no longer an option.*

The Difficult Discussion: Talking to Senior Management, Staff, and Volunteers about Fraud

Studies have shown that many cases involving fraud first involved the chief executive and/or the chief financial officer.[2] The fraud began in these organizations literally at the top. This fact means that board needs first to model the type of ethical behavior that it expects from the rest of the nonprofit. The board and senior executives need to adopt a conflict of interest policy and a code of ethics that includes prohibitions against loans and gifts to management, stringent procedures for travel claims and management of expense accounts, and transparency in dealings. Modeling the behavior is the most effective method of communicating that SOX compliance and ethical behavior is not a fad. Before the board members can talk to the organization about fraud, they need to either augment their current ethical standards or design standards that will address common areas of executive fraud.

Troublesome Areas Related to Fraud

Troublesome areas related to fraud have included:

- *Loans, gifts, bonuses, and perks to executives.* Nonprofit boards often agree to loans and gifts to executives as incentives or as rewards for performance. Nonprofit boards are under much more scrutiny in terms of the way in which they approve executive compensation packages.
- *Excessive compensation and benefits packages.* Congress and state legislatures have taken up the issue of executive compensation because excessive compensation has been a recurring factor in nonprofit scandals.
- *Expense accounts and travel claims.* Financial misappropriation often is hidden in transactions involving expense accounts and travel claims.
- *Lack of an enforceable code of ethics.* Having a code of ethics is not just for show. Members of the board as well as senior executives are *obligated* to conduct themselves according to a code of ethics and need to be

subject to disciplinary measures, including termination, for unethical conduct.

- *Lack of an enforceable conflict of interest policy.* Similarly, a conflict of interest policy should apply to board members and senior management alike.

- *Financially illiterate board members.* Board members are unable to read and interpret financial statements relevant to the nonprofit's operations and investments.

At the very minimum, these issues should be addressed in the nonprofit's human resource policies. Board members lead the way in changing the nonprofit's culture by adopting ethical practices and ensuring that they set the example by their own decisions and actions. Do not expect the rest of the nonprofit's staff and volunteers to change their behavior unless they see that the board has adopted these measures as part of daily operations, and unless they see that the board is willing to hold itself accountable. There must be frank discussion about how important it is for staff and volunteers to report waste, fraud, and abuse.

Why Individuals Are Reluctant to Blow the Whistle on Waste, Fraud, and Abuse

Everyone knows that, despite federal law prohibiting retaliation, whistle-blowing can be a career-limiting gesture. Whistleblowers often discover, despite the egregious financial irregularities that they have identified, that they receive virtually no support from the board or management. The situation is not remedied, and wrongdoers are not held accountable. Subtle negative responses to whistleblowers, such as ostracism or moving the person's office to a less desirable location, can be just as effective as explicit retaliation in silencing or discrediting them.

Whistleblowers are not universally embraced by management in any organization, private or nonprofit. Often they are described as "not team players" or are categorized as troublemakers. Management can use rumor and innuendo to make whistleblowers look bad. *The board needs to send a clear message to management, staff, and volunteers that any kind of negative response to a report of waste, fraud, or abuse is unacceptable.* Whether management approves of the whistleblower's message is irrelevant. The whistleblower protection requirement of SOX is clear about the prohibition against retribution of any kind—even subtle acts. In today's legal environment, the board can be held responsible for "punishing" a whistleblower even in subtle ways. Having an effective whistleblower protection policy is important not only because of the SOX legal requirements, but to provide a mechanism to protect the nonprofit's integrity and future viability.

The board needs to establish a mechanism not only to protect whistleblowers, but to encourage reporting of waste, fraud, or abuse. The sooner that the board and senior management know about a potential problem, the sooner the problem can be handled. Consider whistleblower protection an important factor in your nonprofit's commitment to total quality management. Individuals who report problems with internal controls or procedures should be rewarded. They just saved your nonprofit time, money, and labor. The report might also have identified a problem that, if ignored over time, could result in a crisis.

Factors that Promote Fraud

Fraud and fraudulent activities do not simply happen overnight. Supporting factors within a nonprofit facilitate opportunities for fraud:

- *Motivation.* People have to want to engage in fraudulent activities and believe that there will be few if any consequences if they are ever caught.

- *Occasion for the fraud to take place.* Weak or nonexistent internal controls provide the opportunity to engage in fraudulent activities. Other occasions can include access to petty cash, donations, or other assets that are quickly converted to cash.

- *Sloppy or nonexistent internal controls.* It is easier to cover one's tracks when there are no protocols or records kept.

- *Access to electronic databases and online checking.* Often electronic records will need to be altered to cover the fraud. Individuals who have access to sensitive databases are in a position to set up sham accounts and issue checks to themselves.

- *Organizational culture.* An organizational culture that either denies the possibility of anyone committing fraud or, even more insidious, transforms staff and volunteers into martyrs promotes fraud. How many times have you heard people say, "We work so hard here for so little money." Even more serious is the board's enabling of this dysfunctional attitude: "We pay these people so little, we really can't expect them to agree to these requirements."

- *A board of directors that is asleep at the wheel.* We often hear stories about fraud committed at nonprofit organizations only to learn that the board knew nothing about it and suspected nothing. *That is the single most important reason why the board needs to lead the way in talking about fraud and in instituting and enforcing antifraud measures.*

Sarbanes-Oxley requirements will provide individuals with the opportunity to report waste, fraud, or abuse without fear of retaliation. Document preservation will facilitate more efficient record keeping and provide auditors (external and internal) with better data for their review. The overall strengthening of the internal controls that comes with the implementation of best practices will further reduce the opportunities for fraud and will introduce a change in the organizational culture.

Talking Points in the Discussion about Fraud

The Board needs to lead the way in talking about fraud—and needs to be the visible source of policy making in this area. When the board talks about fraud, it needs to be candid about the factors that support fraud and why the implementation of SOX requirements and best practices will help the nonprofit reduce the potential for fraud within the organization. Managers, staff, and volunteers will need to know that internal controls will either be put in place or upgraded. New policies and procedures will be put in place—and enforced. Compliance with these new measures will become a condition for continued employment.

The board also needs to be resolute in its approach, as it is the entity that will be held responsible for the goings-on in the nonprofit. It is equally important to emphasize that the board is committed to whistleblower protection, and that any type of retaliation is to be reported directly to a designated board member or committee chair.

Do not be sidetracked by the longtime manager, employee, or volunteer whose "feelings will be hurt" if protocols and expectations are changed. The well-being of your nonprofit always comes first! These individuals will just have to get over it if they want to remain part of the nonprofit.

The board's summary message could be: "The board is the ultimate authority in this nonprofit. We are responsible for, and will be held accountable for, what happens in this nonprofit. Therefore, it is our commitment to be in compliance with the Sarbanes-Oxley Act and relevant state legislation. This nonprofit *will* change the way it does business—no excuses. The board is committed to upgrading internal controls and is equally committed to its whistleblower protection policy. We welcome reports of waste, fraud, and abuse, as these types of reports help us to strengthen internal controls. The board commits to protecting whistleblowers from retaliation in any form and would like to hear from any staff or volunteer who feels they have been retaliated against for reporting waste, fraud, or abuse. Please contact [name of board member]."

The Board's Role in Changing the Organization's Culture and Values To Introduce a Platinum Standard

In order to implement Sarbanes-Oxley requirements and best practices, the essence of a nonprofit's culture needs to change. The primary change agents are the board and the senior management team. They begin the process and utilize strategies along the way that bring about a sea change in the way in which a nonprofit does business and looks at its programs, its clients, its donors, its staff, and its future.

The nonprofit's culture is reflected in its values and its belief system, in the ways in which experiences are translated into lessons learned, and in the ways in which new methods are introduced. The board has a number of tools that can be applied to bring about attention and reinforcement to the announced changes. Some of the ways in which the board can highlight the changes that it expects to see—and the consequences for failure to change—include:

- *Change what they articulate as measures of success.* The board controls the metrics for quality. Management, staff, and volunteers will need to adopt a new understanding of quality within the nonprofit. The board needs to present the new quality standards and explain how these standards will be measured.

- *Allocate financial and other resources in a manner that reinforces new values and expected change.* Doing this may require budgetary changes or reordering of priorities, but the message needs to be that the budget will be developed in a way that directly supports implementation of SOX requirements and best practices. Divisions or managers who resist these changes should find that their budgets are reduced or that their division is reorganized to ensure the promotion of managers who support the implementation of best practices. Other resource reallocation can take the form of changing the location of staff workstations or offices. Office "real estate" often comes laden with power implications, and the relocation of an individual's office can convey a powerful message.

- *Change how rewards and consequences are distributed.* It is important to reward the desired behavior and have swift consequences for foot-dragging or outright refusal to comply. It is equally important to present written performance expectations for all staff and volunteers and to document actual performance.
- *Change the rewards.* Change the way in which staff and volunteers are promoted, assigned to plum projects, or awarded special recognition to ensure that these rewards are visibly tied to assisting in the implementation of best practices.

Staff and volunteers need to be able to clearly see the connection between the desired behavior and the positive reinforcement. Their behavior will need to change, but it is equally important that they also see that the behavior of the board has changed as well.

How Implementation of SOX Requirements and Best Practices Facilitates Change

The board's important duties in coordinating SOX compliance and best practices center on coordinating and providing oversight for the whistle-blower protection policy, design of a confidential reporting mechanism and investigation protocols, design of an internal controls review, implementation of a document preservation policy, and prohibitions against destroying documents during an investigation. The implementation of these requirements establishes the framework for implementation of best practices. Exhibit 7.2 presents a checklist for board coordination of SOX compliance and best practices.

EXHIBIT 7.2   BOARD COORDINATION OF SOX COMPLIANCE AND BEST PRACTICES CHECKLIST

☐ Does the board have regular meetings with the nonprofit's senior management? Does the board also have regular meetings in executive session, meaning where staff are not present?

☐ Has the board reviewed the nonprofit's whistleblower protection policy to ensure that it is written in compliance with SOX requirements?

☐ Has the board reviewed the mechanism for whistleblower complaints to be filed to ensure that whistleblowers' rights are preserved? Has the board ensured that all staff and volunteers understand their rights and how to file a report? Has the board designated a board member to serve as a contact for staff and volunteers who believe they have been retaliated against for filing a report?

☐ Has the board directed senior management to put a document preservation policy in place? Has the board set a deadline for this policy to be implemented and has scheduled an informal review of the policy?

☐ Has the board reviewed and approved a policy prohibiting the destruction of documents during an inquiry or legal action?

☐ Has the board conducted (or is planning to conduct in the near future) a review of the nonprofit's internal controls?

☐ Has the board developed a crisis communication plan for the nonprofit?

☐ Has the board ensured that the procedures for all SOX requirements and best practices have been shared with everyone, staff and volunteers alike?

☐ Has the board taken responsibility for conducting unannounced reviews of procedures and protocols to ensure compliance?

Board Oversight and Quality Assurance in Whistleblower Protection

The board should review the nonprofit's policies and procedures on whistleblower protection to ensure that they contain these features:

- *There is a confidential means for reporting suspected waste, fraud, and abuse.* Staff and volunteers need to know how to go about filing the report and what types of evidence they should provide to substantiate their claims.

- *There is a process to investigate any reports thoroughly.* Volunteers and staff should also know how investigations are conducted and what will be expected of them in terms of providing a statement or answering questions.

- *There is a process for disseminating the findings from the investigation.* The whistleblower should also know how the findings of the report will be disseminated.

- *The employee filing the complaint will not be subjected to termination, firing, or harassment, or miss out on promotion.* This is the most important part of the policy. All staff and volunteers should know what their rights are under the whistleblower protection policy.

- *Even if the findings do not support the nature of the complaint, the person who made the complaint will not face any repercussions.* Staff and volunteers also need to understand that if they file a report and the findings do not support their claim, there will not be any repercussions.

Communication is key in ensuring that all employees and volunteers understand why reporting waste, fraud, and abuse is expected, what their rights are, and how investigations are conducted and findings presented. Every employee and volunteer should have a copy of the whistleblower policy, and it should be readily available for review in hard copy and on-line. This policy should also be covered in any orientation or training programs the organization offers for its employees and volunteers. The nonprofit's legal counsel should review the wording of the whistleblower protection policy and provide advice whenever whistleblower reports are filed.

Board Oversight and Quality Assurance in Document Preservation

The board plays a pivotal role in the design, implementation, and maintenance of the nonprofit's document preservation policy. The board should begin the process by reviewing the SOX requirements with its legal counsel and with the nonprofit's senior management. The nonprofit may already have a system in place to track, store, and archive documents. If so, that is great. Begin with the system that you already have in place and expand from there. Electronic documents, including e-mail, word processing documents, databases, and instant messages are also included in the policy. The board's legal counsel and/or financial professional can provide a comprehensive list that suits the needs of your particular organization. Exhibit 7.3 illustrates sample minimum storage requirements.

EXHIBIT 7.3   SAMPLE MINIMUM STORAGE REQUIREMENTS

Document	Storage
Accounts receivable and payable ledgers	7 years
Articles of incorporation, charter, bylaws, minutes	Permanent
Bank reconciliation	3 years
Bank statements, electronic fund transfers, cancelled checks	3 years
Contracts, mortgages, notes, leases (expired)	7 years
Deeds, mortgages, bills of sale	Permanent
Payroll records	7 years
Contracts still in effect	Permanent
Correspondence—legal	Permanent
Correspondence—vendors	2 years
Tax returns and worksheets	Permanent
Grants (funded)	7 years after closure

Source: National Association of Veterans Research and Education Foundations

The written document preservation policy developed by the board must contain these talking points:

- *Describe what the document retention policy is and why it is required by law.* It is important that the staff and volunteers understand that document preservation is a component of SOX that applies to all organizations.
- *Identify what new procedures have emerged from the policy.* Staff and volunteers need to understand how to be in compliance, and what specific actions are required.
- *Identify and explain the obligations of individual staff members and volunteers to ensure that your nonprofit is in compliance.* Requirements for individual staffers and volunteers should be presented in writing. Because this is probably a very new requirement in your organization, the more user-friendly the guidelines, the better.

- *Describe what is expected in terms of new behaviors and procedures and the consequences for individual employees and volunteers who fail to adhere to the new procedures.* It is particularly important that the board be prepared to carry out unpleasant consequences swiftly to send a strong message throughout the organization.

- *Describe when materials should not be destroyed.* Develop a written policy prohibiting destruction of documents when the nonprofit is conducting an investigation or has been ordered to turn over documents, or is in legal proceedings.

- *Identify what documents and records should be preserved and why.*
  - Are the documents paper-only, or are electronic files included? Which ones?
  - What about e-mail and instant messaging?

- *List the expectations about the way in which documents are stored or archived and the ability to retrieve documents.*

- *State how long these documents must be kept.*

- *Describe the protocol for disposing of documents once their storage time has elapsed.*

- *Identify how you can make sure that everyone in the nonprofit—staff and volunteers—understands and adheres to these requirements.*

- *Describe what happens if your nonprofit is in violation.*

The board needs to coordinate the activities in the implementation of a document preservation policy. Since most of today's documents are stored in electronic format, implementing the specifics of the plan can be streamlined. The system you design for document storage, archives, and retrieval must be logical and user-friendly. It is essential that everyone in the organization—from members of the board to the newest clerical staff—what is expected of them. If staff members cannot understand what the policy is about, what is expected of them, and why they are being asked to do this, then the probability of compliance is low.

Technology and Document Preservation

An important companion piece to the document preservation policy is a technology policy. Because the misuse of the nonprofit's technology can create serious liability for the nonprofit, the board needs to design the policy to address the use of all types of technology that are present within the organization. The array of technology includes e-mail, Internet access, voice mail, cell phones, laptops, personal digital assistants (PDAs), faxes, and other equipment owned by the nonprofit. The policy needs to include these talking points:

- Clearly state that all aspects of the nonprofit's technology belong to the nonprofit. There are *no* expectations of personal privacy when using the nonprofit's technology.

- Identify all of the nonprofit's technology—hardware and software, including laptop computers, desktop computers, hand-held devices such as PDAs and BlackBerries, cell phones, Internet access, e-mail, and all software programs purchased through the nonprofit. Be aware that when electronic devices such as laptops or PDAs are "recycled" to another staff member, the "hard drive" of the device may still contain data, documents, or transactions from the previous employee. It is important to institute a procedure to erase the hard drive once all of the documents have been extracted and stored according to your nonprofit's document retention policy.

- Develop a policy on the storage and transportation of sensitive information out of your nonprofit's facilities. Published reports routinely describe the theft of laptops containing sensitive data. The same thing could happen to your nonprofit if you store sensitive information about donors, clients, or staff on laptops that leave your premises.

All staff and volunteers need to be briefed on the technology policy, receive a copy of the policy, and sign a letter stating that they have been briefed on the nonprofit's technology policy and pledge to comply with it. Appendix D has a sample of the procedures for implementing a technology policy. Exhibit 7.4 presents a technology policy checklist.

Your Nonprofit's Web Site

Your nonprofit's Web site is the electronic "face" of your organization. The way in which it is designed, its features (which make it user-friendly or not), and the content say important things about your organization. Some nonprofits utilize their Web sites to collect donations, sell merchan-

---

EXHIBIT 7.4   TECHNOLOGY POLICY CHECKLIST

☐ Does your technology policy state that all of the nonprofit's technology belongs to the nonprofit? Do staff and volunteers understand that there are *no* expectations of personal privacy when using the nonprofit's technology?

☐ Do staff and volunteers know that e-mail and web access belong to the nonprofit?

☐ Do users of e-mail understand the nonprofit's policy on inappropriate e-mail messages, which include:

- Jokes
- Harassment
- Political commentary, particularly hate messages
- Anything you would not want to read on the front page of your local newspaper or have CNN broadcast

☐ Does your technology policy address all of the nonprofit's technology—hardware and software, including laptop computers, desktop computers, hand-held devices (i.e., PDAs and BlackBerries) cell phones, Internet access, e-mail, and all software programs purchased through the nonprofit?

☐ All electronic devices, such as laptops and PDAs, must be returned to the nonprofit when leaving its employ or volunteer assignment.

☐ The nonprofit has a policy on the storage and transportation of sensitive information on laptops that leave the premises.

☐ Everyone entrusted with the nonprofit's electronics understands that they will be held personally accountable for the safety of the equipment, the safe use of the equipment, and the security of the data that is stored within these electronics.

---

dise, or respond to a global disaster. The nonprofit's document preservation policy should also discuss those "documents" that can be pages on the Web site such as:

- Your nonprofit's 990s for the past three years
- Documents that demonstrate SOX compliance and best practices, such as your nonprofit's whistleblower protection policy and document preservation policy
- Reports, information about board members, programs, annual reports, and financial reports

Security is rapidly becoming one of the most significant challenges to Web sites—all Web sites, nonprofit or private sector. Nonprofit Web sites need to have firewalls and encryption software to protect donor information and to ensure that online transactions with donors are secure. When donors put a credit card number on your Web site, they and you need to feel confident that this sensitive information is properly encrypted and transported to the correct location. You should also consider including information for donors about how to safely make a donation. For example, include recommendations on the website for safety in online transactions, such as using a credit card rather than a debit card, checking credit card statements to ensure that all the transactions are accurate. If possible, include a link to your local Better Business Bureau, chamber of commerce, or non-profit clearinghouse to verify that you are a member in good standing.

THE BOARD'S OVERSIGHT ROLE IN IMPLEMENTING YOUR NONPROFIT'S DOCUMENT PRESERVATION POLICY

In today's legal and legislative environment, nonprofit boards are being held as the ultimate authority in all of the nonprofit's operations. This higher standard of accountability is the catalyst for board action in ensuring that the nonprofit is compliant with the SOX requirement for establishing a document preservation policy and implementing a prohibition against destroying documents during an investigation or legal action.

The board needs to create a cross-functional team representing each division within the nonprofit. Each member of the team should be tasked with being that functional area's document manager. The individual's performance expectations would be altered to reflect the new responsibilities. This person should be tasked with coordinating the document preservation policy components that apply to his or her department. It is essential that all document managers have the same training and knowledge of organizational systems and technology, such as scanners, software, and the like, to ensure that documents are selected, preserved, archived, and able to be retrieved in a consistent, standardized manner.

Establish rules for appropriate and secure electronic transmission of sensitive materials. Work with information technology and legal professionals to ensure that these rules are comprehensive and appropriate to your nonprofit.

The board must oversee the development of retention rules (based on legal requirements and the operational needs of your nonprofit) and ensure that these rules are clearly disseminated to all staff and volunteers. A security classification system must be developed (a simple one is fine) that allows for documents to be classified as "confidential," "private," or other designation that prevents general access.

The board needs to ensure that a directive against destruction of documents that are part of an investigation is written and distributed throughout the organization. The team also needs to review and approve rules for managing, storing, preserving, and archiving electronic messages and other electronic data. The rules should list the types of documents that are to be retained and how these documents are to be stored.

Last, the board needs to conduct routine audits of the document retention system, generally on an unannounced basis. The findings of these audits will provide the team with valuable insight into the quality of the current protocols, the degree to which staff members are in compliance, and what midcourse corrections are necessary to achieve full compliance.

The board needs to ensure that the document preservation system is logical and user-friendly. If staff members cannot understand what the policy is about, what is expected of them, and why they are being asked to do this, the probability of success is low. The document preservation policy is one area in which the board must aggressively supervise management and staff to ensure that the system is put into place, is operational, and is maintained. The board should consider directing management and staff either to modify the current system or implement a new system using the streamlined approach described in the next six steps.

Step 1.   Consider what types of documents your nonprofit needs to store/ archive and be able to retrieve. Some examples of documents that need to be stored include:

- Contracts with vendors for services, including insurance policies and auditor contracts (particularly to demonstrate that the auditing firm is not providing any other services to your nonprofit)
- Contracts with external clients (i.e., public sector agencies) to provide services to the nonprofit's external clients
- Contracts with your nonprofit's programmatic clients
- Contracts with your nonprofit's management, staff, and volunteers (if applicable)

- Documents that a regulatory agency requires you to retain, such as tax returns, business license documents, vehicle registration forms, and professional licensure documents

- Correspondence with regulators about your nonprofit's operations

- Documents containing information that a regulator would need to review

- Documents required by local, state, and federal law and correspondence regarding these documents

- Documents that have historical, legal, or programmatic significance for your nonprofit

- Instant messages or e-mail that contain negotiations for a contract or other legal agreement

- Any document that would provide proof that your nonprofit took action in a business, contractual, or legal matter

- Financial documents, reports, analyses, and forecasts.

- Donor records, history, and correspondence

- Human resources records, including volunteer and board files

- Documents that reflect the sale of property, merchandise, or any tangible or intangible assets

The board needs to review the requirements of any third-party reviewers, such as auditors or regulatory agencies, to ensure that your nonprofit's system will satisfy the expectations of these reviewers. These requirements can be easily obtained from the IRS, legal counsel, and your nonprofit's banker or other financial professional.

Step 2. Direct management to inventory the nonprofit's current record system to determine what records are in use, what records are in storage, and what records are archived. This step should also include a review of the types of e-mail messages and instant messages that are routinely transmitted along with attachments. The board needs to review the findings of this step.

Step 3. Direct management to develop retention rules (based on legal requirements and the operational needs of your nonprofit), and ensure that these rules are clearly disseminated to all staff and volunteers. Develop a simple classification system that allows for documents to be classified as "confidential," "private," or other designation that precludes them from general access. As part of this step, it is essential to develop a training program for staff to ensure that they understand what is expected of them, what the procedures are, and what records they are expected to retain. The board needs to review and approve of these rules.

Step 4. Direct management to develop a process for finding and preserving documents that either will be or are part of an investigation or legal action. There must also be a mechanism for announcing that no documents are to be destroyed until an "all clear" notice is given—and stiff consequences for failing to adhere to this directive. The board needs to review and approve of these procedures.

Step 5. Direct management to develop rules for managing, storing, preserving, and archiving electronic messages or other electronic data. The rules should list the types of documents that are to be retained and how these documents are to be stored. The process need not be complicated, but the rules need to be standardized; there is no room for "doing your own thing." Staff and volunteers need to understand that they are obligated to adhere to the rules or face the consequences. The rules should also include steps to be taken to ensure that the documents cannot be tampered with, such as using pdf files or passwords. It is particularly important to store financial records in such a way as to ensure that they represent a true and honest picture of the nonprofit's financial profile and/or other financial description. Regulators will expect to be able to rely on the accuracy of all of your electronic records, and the board will be held accountable if there is a failure in this process. The board needs to review and approve the rules for managing, storing, preserving, and archiving electronic messages.

The nonprofit's technology policy is an important component of this step.

- Direct management to ensure that all of the materials documenting the staff/volunteer briefings are stored and archived. Copies of the letters that staff and volunteers signed acknowledging

their receipt of a written copy of the policy and their commitment to be in compliance need to be stored in their personnel
files. If volunteers do not have personnel files, such files must be
developed and the letters need to be stored or scanned into the
database.

- Direct management to develop a working inventory of all of
the nonprofit's technology, which is updated on a daily or
weekly basis if necessary. The board treasurer should receive
monthly inventory reports, as the sum total value of these assets
can be considerable. The inventory should include hardware
and software, including laptop computers, desktop computers,
hand-held devices such as PDAs and BlackBerries, cell phones,
Internet access, e-mail, and all software programs purchased
through the nonprofit. Be aware that when electronic devices
such as laptops or PDAs are "recycled" to another staff member, the "hard drive" of the device may still contain data,
documents or transactions from the previous employee. It is
important to institute a procedure to erase the hard drive once
all of the documents have been extracted and stored according
to your nonprofit's Document Retention Policy.

- Develop a policy on the storage and transportation of sensitive
information out of your nonprofit's facilities. Published reports
describe multiple scenarios of laptops of bank employees being
stolen that contained client financial data. The same thing
could happen to your nonprofit if you store sensitive information about donors, clients, or staff on laptops that leave your
premises.

- State that when an employee leaves his/her job at the nonprofit
s/he will be expected to surrender all technology to the HR department prior to his/her departure—and obtain a signed receipt
from HR for all of the equipment that was turned over to HR.

Assign specific employees within each division of your nonprofit
the responsibility and the requisite power and resources for document retention within their division. It is essential that these individuals all have the same training and knowledge of organizational
systems and technology, such as scanners, software, and the like, to

ensure that documents are selected, preserved, and archived, and able to be retrieved in a consistent, standardized manner.

Establish rules for appropriate and secure electronic transmission of sensitive materials. Work with information technology and legal professionals to ensure that these rules are comprehensive and appropriate to your nonprofit.

Does your nonprofit have a privacy policy that relates to donor information? What about information about clients, staff, volunteers? If not, you need to institute privacy policies for donors, clients, staff, and volunteers immediately and disseminate the policy(ies) to these constituencies. For example, if your nonprofit has a Web site, do you list the names of donors? If you list these names, have each of the donors signed a consent document? In today's world of identity theft and Internet hacking, it is particularly important to protect donors, staff, and board members.

Step 6. The board must develop a means by which the document preservation system will be audited on a regular basis to ensure that all staff members are in compliance with the provisions. If at all possible, retaining an independent third party to conduct the audits would render higher-quality results. Management and staff should understand that the audits will be random and unannounced. Consequences for noncompliance should be meted out quickly to send a message to the entire organization. Understand that your nonprofit is a *business*; you need to conduct operations in a businesslike fashion. Today's higher standards of board accountability means that your board has an obligation to your donors, your clients, and your staff to ensure that your organization is in compliance with this component of SOX legislation. It is not just a "best practice"; it is the *law*, and it applies to all organizations in this country, including your nonprofit.

THE BOARD'S ROLE IN THE REVIEW OF INTERNAL CONTROLS

A review of internal controls is designed to take a current reading of your nonprofit's policies and procedures. For example, does your nonprofit have policies to prevent or deter fraud or misappropriation of funds or other assets? The board's oversight of the process is intended to identify those areas that need attention and upgrade. The extent to which the internal controls in your organization need upgrading and the importance of the individual functions to your nonprofit's operations will determine the schedule for these activities. The important issue in this process is the recognition that your organization will not be able to adopt the SOX best practices fully until your infrastructure is positioned to make it happen.

How might the board take the first steps in ensuring that the nonprofit's internal controls are consistent with SOX standards? Discuss the role of the audit committee and the nonprofit's key external advisors in crafting a strategy to review and upgrade the nonprofit's current internal controls. The board can assign the audit committee the task of initiating a review of the internal controls. Steps for this process can be found in Appendix E.

A Platinum Standard for the Board

In order for the board to be effective in introducing a platinum standard to the nonprofit's management, staff, and volunteers, the board must model a platinum operating standard. Platinum standards encompass all that the board does, from recruiting and screening potential members, to board orientations, to conducting board meetings, to ensuring that the entire board is apprised of important financial and/or operational information that is generated from the staff. Appendix F contains samples of materials for board governance, administration. and performance expectations.

Board Meetings

The beginning of a new platinum standard starts with the way in which board meetings are conducted and documented. Conducting board meetings is one of the obligations of the board's executive committee. The executive committee should ensure that the staff members have prepared the materials that are necessary and sufficient to assist board members in coming to the meeting prepared. The executive committee also needs to ensure that board members actually come prepared to discuss and vote on the topics listed on the agenda.

The agenda should reflect the necessary components of a board meeting:

- Date and time that the meeting takes place
- Minutes from the previous meeting. The minutes of the meeting should also be complete in terms of the motions that were seconded and carried in the meeting.
- Topics to be addressed in the meeting—and the amount of time that will be devoted to each. The board chair needs to *enforce* the time limitations so that the meeting begins and ends on time.
- Opportunity for questions on materials that were sent to board members in advance of the meeting. Committee and staff reports should be prepared in advance and included in board members' packets. The executive's report and the financial reports may need to be discussed at length to ensure that board members are fully informed about the financial status of the nonprofit.

Robert's Rules of Order should be adopted in a manner that introduces stability and civility into board meetings.

The board chair should at all times be firmly in control of the discussion and the agenda. Board members and/or staff should *never* be permitted to hijack the meeting to suit their individual agendas. If discussions are going on at length, the board chair has an obligation to intervene to table a discussion or move to the next item on the agenda.

Board Orientations

Board orientations should also include a detailed description of the SOX best practices adopted by your nonprofit's board. Although the board orientation addresses a wide range of topics, it is important to ensure that all board members understand what the SOX best practices are and why they are essential to remaining faithful to the board's three legal standards: care, loyalty, and obedience. Each best practice should be described in detail that explains its role and function in keeping the nonprofit's operations transparent.

An important topic in the board orientation is the conflict of interest policy and the code of ethics. Both of these policies should be examined in greater detail and presented to new and current board members. Board members should understand what is expected of them and why it is essential for the board and senior management to adhere to the conflict of interest policy and the code of ethics. Providing board members with sample conflict of interest statements and reviewing policy documents will serve to reinforce the message. Another way of clarifying expectations is to have a member of the board provide an example of the nonprofit's conflict of interest letter, which may or may not have any disclosures. Appendix G contains samples of a conflict-of-interest policy and annual letter.

Give examples of how a board member may use the code of ethics as a resource for decision-making. Appendix H has a sample code of ethics. Board members should be directed to consider whether the outcomes are in the best interest of the nonprofit and are free of any personal or professional gain on the individual's part. Both the conflict of interest policy and the code of ethics are tools for effective decision making. The board orientation is one of the occasions in which the best practices can be illustrated as rubrics for responsible governance. Board meetings, board retreats, and other working meetings present opportunities to remind members about the nonprofit's commitment to transparency.

Appendix F contains samples of materials that all board members should have in a binder. The binder should include:

- The nonprofit's mission and vision statements
- The nonprofit's strategic plan
- Brief history of the nonprofit
- Financial statements from the past three months
- Development and fundraising profile of the agency
- Board member legal duties: care, loyalty, obedience
- Board policies:
  - Meeting attendance and preparation expectations
  - Fiduciary obligations and conflict of interest policies
  - Financial support of the nonprofit
  - Code of ethics
  - Conflict of interest policy
  - Committee structure (if applicable)
- Board roster
- Staff roster

PLATINUM STANDARDS AND SOX BEST PRACTICES

SOX best practices are designed to enhance the completeness and reliability of your nonprofit's internal operations as well as ensure that the organization is in regulatory compliance. To review, SOX best practices include:

- *Appointment of an audit committee* whose role is to oversee the annual audit or financial review (for small nonprofits) and to upgrade the financial literacy of the board. The audit committee is the link between the board and its auditor or financial reviewer. This committee is an important element in ensuring that the board understands the results of the annual audit or financial review (for small nonprofits) and that the board's skills in reading and interpreting financial statements is kept up to date. The intent of this best practice is the complete independence of the auditor and the audit committee. This means that if the person who is currently conducting the nonprofit's audit or financial review also prepares the nonprofit's IRS 990 form, then the individual must divest him- or herself from one of these roles. The intent of SOX legislation is to segregate these duties. An auditor or auditing firm that provides services to a nonprofit in addition to conducting an audit presents a conflict of interest.

- *Certified financial statements.* The nonprofit's board is ultimately accountable for the accuracy and integrity of the nonprofit's financial statements and IRS 990 forms. The board needs to ensure that the nonprofit's executive director, chief executive officer (CEO), or chief financial officer (CFO) can validate the accuracy of the nonprofit's financial statements. "For a nonprofit organization, CEO and CFO sign-off on financial statements would not carry the weight of law [unless it is required under state law], but it would signal the importance that the CEO, in particular, pays to understanding the nonprofit's financial condition . . . . Signing off on the financial statements provides formal assurance that both the CEO and CFO have reviewed them carefully and stand by them."[3]

- *Enhanced detail and accuracy in the preparation of IRS tax documents in the annual submission of IRS 990 filings.* Failure to submit a 990 is no longer an option.

- *A higher level of board accountability*, including upgraded policies and procedures for board member recruitment, board orientation, performance expectations and adherence to legal principles of governance.

- *Conflict of interest policy* that facilitates greater focus on decision making for the good of the nonprofit.

- *Code of ethics* for board and senior management that preludes any loans to directors, officers, management, or staff of the nonprofit.

- *Internal controls*, particularly as these relate to financial operations, and compliance with all laws and regulations at the federal, state, and local level.

- *Transparency at all levels of management, including the board*, and in all transactions, including travel claims and reimbursements. The board needs to insist that there are written procedures for filing travel and reimbursement claims and that these procedures are enforced, even by means of unannounced audits.

- *Consistent adherence to new policies and procedures and enforcement of the policies.* The board will not be successful in its endeavors to bring the nonprofit into compliance unless the new policies and procedures are enforced. In many nonprofits, two of the most prominent areas of operations are finance and document retention. These areas garner significant attention because the ways in which reports are developed and documents retained can indicate how honest the nonprofit is being in conducting its operations and how committed it is to transparency and full disclosure. Documents such as Form 990 are among the new ways of fully disclosing financial operations and position to the public. Form 990 is not just for tax reporting anymore. The public has easy access to Form 990s online through organizations such as GuideStar. Using an organization's Form 990, interested parties can track the sources and uses of its funds. Form 990s can also indicate that all major transactions are in compliance with other SOX expectations, such as avoidance of even the appearance of a conflict of interest.

The nonprofit's commitment to adopting and maintaining SOX best practices can be demonstrated in a review of internal controls. The process and outcomes can be used to measure the progress that your nonprofit has made in the development of the platinum standard.

Compliance cannot simply be a rote operation; the nonprofit must demonstrate that the commitment to excellence transcends all levels and is evident in all operational systems and in the symbiotic relationship that exists among the various systems within the organization.

Board members need to fully participate in the implementation of platinum operating standards by examining their own behavior and commitment. Here are some platinum standards that board members need to individually adopt:

- *Attend board meetings on a regular basis.* Board members who do not attend meetings regularly have only a marginal understanding of the nonprofit's operational, financial, and governance issues. These board members are poor representatives of the nonprofit and, in their lack of knowledge, can make unwise decisions.

- *Understand their governance role.* Board members, by the legal standards of care, loyalty, and obedience, are expected to put the welfare of the nonprofit ahead of any personal consideration and certainly ahead of any personal gain. Board members are not there to micromanage the nonprofit, nor are they simply "window dressing" for senior management's agenda.

- *Read and understand (or ask questions until they obtain clarity) all materials sent in advance of a board meeting.* The operative expectation is that board members come to board meetings prepared to ask questions or obtain clarity because they have carefully reviewed all of the materials in advance.

- *Review financial documents carefully and provide appropriate oversight.* Board members are expected either to understand the financial documents or to seek assistance in learning how to read and interpret financial statements. In the area of financial operations, board members need to ask the difficult questions and insist on appropriate financial materials.

- *Disclose any real or potential conflicts of interest.* Board members, in order to adhere to the standard of loyalty, must disclose any real or potential conflicts of interest to the board. The rest of the board needs to know about these real or potential conflicts of interest so that steps can be taken to eliminate their impact on board deliberations and decisions.

- *Adhere to a code of ethics.* Board members need to adhere to a code of ethics that spells out the nonprofit's values and principles. Adherence to a code of ethics is another way in which board members put the interest and well-being of the nonprofit ahead of their own.

Summary

The board plays a pivotal role in ushering in a platinum operating standard for the nonprofit. This role presumes that all board members are willing to begin this transformation at the top: with board practices. It is important for the board to change its operating standards and values to correspond with the quality and expectations of SOX requirements and best practices.

The board also has a role in ensuring that the nonprofit introduces and executes SOX requirements and best practices. As these measures are introduced to the nonprofit, the board must ensure that all staff and volunteers are briefed on what is expected and how the way they conduct business needs to change. Once the changes are in place, the board needs to continue its vigilance to ensure that the requirements and best practices are incorporated into the organization's operational design.

Endnotes

1. Johnson, 2004.
2. COSO, 1999.
3. www.guidestar.org.

CHAPTER 8

SOX and the Really Small Nonprofit Board

Susan is a member of a tiny nonprofit board. Her nonprofit provides dance education to people of all ages. It is a grassroots organization committed to introducing the joys of dance to young and old alike. Susan worries that the expectations of the public sector and the nonprofit world will serve to wipe out the dance center. In her community, there are virtually no other nonprofits providing this type of service to such a wide-ranging clientele. At a recent seminar, the speaker informed Susan that an audit would cost her nonprofit approximately $5,000. He might just as well have said $1 million.

Although Bob is 3,000 miles away, he finds himself in a situation similar to Susan's. His nonprofit is only a few years old. Already the young people that his nonprofit serves have won awards for excellence in their artistry. Yet the nascent infrastructure of his nonprofit needs to catch up with the needs of its clients and the growth potential that their talent offers.

Both Bob and Susan need a way to incorporate the SOX best practices on a scale that fits their nonprofits.

This chapter offers recommendations for nonprofit boards of prelaunch or start-up nonprofits. All of the techniques, methods, and recommendations discussed in the previous seven chapters can be scaled to fit very small nonprofit boards. Small boards are particularly vulnerable to the same problems found in larger boards, but can also become overwhelmed if the nonprofit attracts a large grant or other types of funding. By incorporating SOX requirements and best practices at an early stage, small nonprofits can reinforce their organizational "framework" to sustain growth spurts.

CHALLENGES OF REALLY SMALL BOARDS

Small or start-up nonprofits often have a grassroots structure. They were formed to address a particular cause or passion, but in their initial stages they are constrained in terms of financial and human capital resources. Additionally, these nonprofits have boards that are dealing with these types of challenges:

- They have a limited ability to attract solid board members, particularly those with specific skill sets, contacts, and financial resources. Financial literacy can be a significant problem in these boards.

- The grassroots model is often ineffective in assembling a board that is up to the challenges of today's legal and legislative expectations.

- The operation may have only one or two paid staff members or only part-time staff.

- The nonprofit's working paradigm is either counterculture or resistant to incorporating best practices from the private sector for fear of appearing to "sell out" to the establishment.

- The founder of the nonprofit is an integral part of the organization's management and governance. The individual may be the local saint for pursuing the cause, but he or she does not understand the boundaries between management and governance and expects the board to rubber-stamp all ideas.

FIVE MYTHS THAT HOLD SMALL NONPROFITS BACK

Myth #1. We are poor, grassroots, small, not part of the "establishment," out in the boonies [or other reasons, just fill in the blank]. The litany of woes goes on forever. The reality is that in the eyes of the law, your nonprofit is accountable for its operations and outcomes.

Myth #2. No one would investigate us, sue us, or [fill in the action]. The truth of the matter is that the United States Senate Finance Committee is considering scores of regulations that would require nonprofits to comply with new laws and regulations. For example, one proposal was for all nonprofits to have their 501(c)(3) designations reviewed every five years by the Internal Revenue Service.

Myth #3. We are not Enron. We do not have time to worry about laws. Our staff and board suffer so much and are so underappreciated that we barely can get through another year. The truth is that we have now entered the twenty-first century. Your nonprofit *does* have to comply with federal and state laws—all of them. If you and your staff/board really feel that way, you need to consider closing your nonprofit or finding a fresh and energetic staff or board.

Myth #4. SOX best practices are expensive and time-consuming. There are many ways in which a small nonprofit can incorporate SOX best practices into its operations. Most of these best practices take the form of policies and procedures. The appendixes contain samples of a range of policies and documents. The most important and powerful change that a small nonprofit would have to make is in its collective mind-set. Establishing a schedule or sequence of deliverables is essential in helping a nonprofit stay on track.

Myth #5. If we insist on board member productivity, no one will join the board. If your nonprofit is having difficulty recruiting board members because you demand performance, then you are recruiting the wrong type of people. Effective board members are not afraid of work, nor are they looking for the path of least resistance. By the way, they will ask you if your nonprofit has directors and officers insurance, and they will not join your board unless you secure this insurance.

Actively embracing a mind-set that recognizes the nonprofit as a legitimate business entity is healthy for all concerned. The nonprofit may be small in size but can be as large in spirit as any large nonprofit. The time has come for *all* nonprofits to understand that the public sector and the public at large expect accountability and responsible management. Small nonprofits are expected to be fully accountable to their donors, their community and to the law. The days of nonprofits evading accountability for their board actions, operations and handling of finances are over!

How to Scale SOX Best Practices in Small Nonprofits

Your nonprofit will not always be small—and it is easier to have built "strong bones" in the early days of the organization. The adaptation of SOX best practices serves to illustrate the nonprofit's commitment to maintaining public trust and serving its mission. Further, having these policies and procedures in place illustrates to current and potential donors that the nonprofit's board and management are committed to the organization as a going concern.

SOX best practices will help your board and senior management to grow your nonprofit into a larger organization. Demonstrating that your nonprofit is willing to be accountable will help attract the resources that your organization needs. The providers of these resources need to be confident that your nonprofit is a good "investment" of their funds, or time, or in-kind donation. Every nonprofit, even a small one, has an obligation to its donors, clients, and community at large to safeguard the organization's assets and make decisions that will support its mission. Board development and training in financial literacy are wise investments of time and energy—and money if necessary.

Consider the ways in which each recommendation can be scaled to suit the needs of the small nonprofit. How might your nonprofit be able to adapt these requirements to fit your organization's size?

Whistleblower Protection Policy

A whistleblower protection policy is one of two Sarbanes-Oxley requirements that apply to all organizations—right now. This policy is not size sensitive. Once the policy is in place and approved by the board, everyone in the organization must be advised that it exists and what the procedure is for filing a report or grievance related to waste, fraud, and abuse. Appendix B has a sample of the talking points that need to be in a whistleblower protection policy.

Document Retention and Storage Protocols

An document retention program, which includes a prohibition of destroying documents to be used in an investigation, is the second Sarbanes-Oxley requirement that applies to all organizations. This policy is, again, not necessarily size sensitive. In a small nonprofit, the key for document retention is to keep the process very simple. The plan can be enlarged as the nonprofit grows. The initial process should focus on financial documents, legal documents, and human resources documents. Training for staff and volunteers needs to be very simple and user-friendly. People will ignore complicated processes, and you can hardly blame them for doing that. People simply have too much to do. Smaller organizations might consider establishing a streamlined, four-step sequence for activities that relate to document retention, such as:

1. Draft a *brief* policy with simple, easily understood language that prohibits the destruction of documents while the nonprofit is under investigation or in other crisis scenarios. The policy need not be lengthy, just a statement that in the event of an investigation or crisis, a general order will be circulated that prohibits the destruction of any documents. Failure to comply can result in termination. Important! It is essential that your nonprofit is prepared to execute the consequences that it states in a policy like this. If your nonprofit is not prepared to terminate someone for violation of this policy, do not include language to that effect.

2. Develop a list of all of the types of documents that need to be stored and archived. It is particularly important to store those documents that provide proof that something was done or negotiated, that a contract was written for [name of vendor], or that support actions. Legal documents, personnel files, board files, and volunteer files are important to store and archive. Here are some types of documents that your nonprofit probably has in its files:
   - Financial documents—reports, analysis, and forecasts
   - Donor records—history and correspondence
   - Human resource records—personnel records, contracts
   - Documents reflecting the sale of property, goods, or other tangible assets
   - Documents that a regulatory agency requires or are required by law
   - Documents containing information that an auditor would need to review

- Contracts with vendors or other providers of products or services
- Client files
- Donor files
- Proposals prepared in response to requests for proposals (RFPs)
- Documents related to your nonprofit's operations or that have historic, legal, or programmatic significance
- E-mail or instant messages that contain negotiations for a contract, Memorandum of Understanding (MOU), or other legal agreements
- Documents related to a mortgage or lease or other real estate transaction
- Any document that would provide proof that your nonprofit took action in a business, contractual, or legal matter

3. *Establish a user-friendly process for retrieving documents.* The storage protocols need to be very simple. Documents need to be easily retrieved because regulatory agencies auditing your nonprofit want documents immediately.

4. *Do a test-run of the protocols.* Do they work? Can they be simpler and easier to understand?

If your review of Steps 1 through 4 indicates that you have to clean up your nonprofit's files, consider this a gift. Your nonprofit will function better when it is easy to store and retrieve documents.

Audit Committee

For many nonprofits, the cost of an audit is prohibitive. For example, if the nonprofit's budget is below $2 million, an audit may be too expensive. However, the nonprofit's financial statements and procedures must be evaluated to determine that the nonprofit is in good financial health. Your nonprofit's finance committee can become a finance/audit committee to make certain that the organization's financial statements and processes are evaluated. If possible, recruit one or two individuals who are not on the board—and not going to join the board—to do a short "Financial Evaluation" project. How can this be done? Here are some suggestions:

- *Find an intern from a local university.* The members of the financial evaluation team can work with the intern to generate a review of the nonprofit's books and internal controls. Many graduate tax or finance programs offer internship opportunities for students who would like to become auditors. This is a potential win-win situation. Your nonprofit receives cutting-edge services (the intern is usually supervised by a professor who is a CPA), and the graduate student can list the internship on his or her resume. Your nonprofit, as the provider of a *professional opportunity* for a graduate student, can afford to be choosy. When inquiring, insist that the intern be an excellent student (with a GPA of at least 3.5) and insist on proof of the student's academic excellence (whether in the form of a transcript or a recommendation from the dean). Before the student is placed, review the internship "contract" with the university. Insist that you be provided with contact information for the professor who is supervising the internship. The financial evaluation team from the finance/audit committee, the professor, and the student can tailor the internship to meet your nonprofit's needs.

- *Contact the local chapter of the CPA society.* Professionals such as CPAs and attorneys often are required to provide pro bono services to the community.

- *Request assistance from a local nonprofit clearinghouse.* Nonprofit clearinghouses can often put smaller nonprofits in contact with service providers.

Financial Literacy Training for Board and Senior Management

Financial literacy training can be provided by your banker, accountant or other financial professional. Graduate students can also provide financial literacy training. The training can be done independently or can be part of an internship, particularly if the graduate student is interested in a teaching career. A phone call to the placement office or internship office at your local college or university can connect you with individuals who could provide these services.

Another way to obtain this type of training is to ask your banker to do a presentation or contact a nonprofit clearinghouse. Again, it is essential to keep the training simple and user-friendly. The handouts should not be complex, and board members should be able to use these materials as resources.

Conflict of Interest Policy

All nonprofits, no matter what their size, should have in place a conflict-of-interest policy. Having a conflict-of-interest policy serves the dual purpose of educating the board on its legal obligation of "loyalty" and on what constitutes a "conflict of interest." Some board members are very reluctant to be forthcoming about real or potential conflicts of interest for fear that they will be dismissed from the board. Dismissal does not have to happen. A board member can disclose a conflict of interest and continue to be a productive and useful member. Educating the board is essential, and having a plan to deal judiciously with any disclosed conflicts of interest will help to encourage more transparency.

This policy and set of procedures are easily drafted for nonprofits of any size. Appendix G contains a sample conflict-of-interest policy and letter. Consider preparing a policy and set of procedures that deal with the major areas of concern. For example, it is essential that all board and senior management sign a letter disclosing any real or potential conflicts of interest. If the board member or staff member has no conflicts of interest, this also should be signified on the letter. The letters need to be kept on file and archived (see document preservation section). The conflict-of-interest policy itself needs to be distributed, and all board members and senior staff members need to initial or sign a form (which could be one form that captures all of the initials or signatures) stating that they have received a copy of the policy.

More important, everyone on the board and all senior staff need to understand that disclosure is the expected norm and that failing to disclose a real or potential conflict of interest is grounds for dismissal. The board can institute simple procedures for excusing a board member or senior staff member when the discussion addresses an area in which the individual indicated a conflict of interest. The procedures need not be onerous or complicated, just standardized so everyone is treated alike.

Code of Ethics for Board and Senior Management

This policy describes the types of behavioral expectations that relate to the roles of board members and members of senior management. One provision that is particularly significant is the prohibition against any type of loan or financial gift by the nonprofit to a board member or member of the staff at any level. Nonprofits of all sizes should have a code of ethics. It need not be lengthy or complex. A sample code of ethics is in Appendix H.

Board Policies and Procedures

This document outlines the *size of the board* and *the various roles and duties of the board*, including the distinction between governance roles and management roles within the nonprofit. The document also includes a *summary of board committees' descriptions and performance objectives* and the *board's self-evaluation process*. Samples of materials to help you present a board orientation can be found in Appendix F.

KEYS TO SUCCESS IN CUSTOMIZING SOX BEST PRACTICES

There is no reason why small nonprofits should not be able to adopt all of the Sarbanes-Oxley best practices. Perhaps the most important aspect of embarking on this endeavor is to understand that any best practice can be customized to address the nonprofit's size, scope, and operations. It can be done, and there are people in your community who would be willing to help—universities, professional organizations, and nonprofit clearinghouses. You simply have to ask for assistance.

Board development in small nonprofit organizations is particularly important. Here are some recommendations to establish a solid strategy for strengthening your small board and preparing it to grow and thrive in the years to come.

- *Develop an organizational resolve to strengthen your nonprofit's infrastructure.* Consider the ways in which best practices can be tailored to fit your nonprofit. . . . Your nonprofit is only small in size (at the moment), but can have a spirit, drive and commitment equal to any large nonprofit.

- *Bring on at least one new board member this year.* Target your recruitment to members who bring a needed skill set, such as finance, to the board. Today's nonprofit boards, even really small ones, cannot afford to be populated with individuals who are passive and/or lack the requisite skills—and assertiveness—to provide appropriate governance and oversight to the nonprofit. It is important, however, to have your legal counsel and insurance professional be independent of the board.

- *Create a scaled-down committee system that deals with essentials,* such as oversight for financial management and an annual financial review instead of an audit.

- *Utilize board meetings, board retreats, and staff meetings to present information on SOX best practices, the legislative environment, and, if applicable, any state laws on nonprofit accountability.* The more the board, management, and staff understand about accountability expectations, the more they will understand how important it is to invest in adopting SOX best practices.

- *Institute whistleblower protection (SOX Requirement).* It is important that the nonprofit have a whistleblower protection policy for all staff and volunteers and enforce it without exception. This policy is required regardless of the size of the nonprofit.

- *Institute a document preservation policy (SOX Requirement).* Establish a system that documents the policies that are in place and the methods for enforcement, and enforce it.

- *Demand financial literacy.* Financial literacy is essential for all board members regardless of the size of the board. The executive director (ED) and chief financial officer (CFO) need to be able to certify the accuracy of financial documents and other submissions, such as 990 forms. It is essential that all members of the board are fully aware of the financial condition of the organization and that senior executives, such as the ED and the CFO, are able to sign without hesitation

- *Establish a code of ethics for board and senior management—prohibition of inside dealings.* This policy needs to be in place regardless of the size of the board. The board needs to adopt a policy strictly prohibiting personal loans to any director or officer and a human resources policy that prohibits lending money to board members, the chief executive officer, ED, CFO, or other staff member. This policy describes the types of behavioral expectations that relate to the roles of board member and member of senior management. One provision that is particularly significant is the prohibition against any type of loan or financial gift by the nonprofit to a board member or member of the staff at any level. No exceptions should *ever* be made to these policies.

- *Institute a conflict-of-interest policy.* Regardless of the size of the board, all board members are obligated to act in a manner consistent with their legal obligations of care, loyalty, and obedience. The individual board member is not "guilty" of anything by disclosing that he or she has a potential conflict of interest. Actually, this type of disclosure is something to be applauded. The important next step is to have the potential conflict of interest documented via a "conflict-of-interest statement" that all board members—and senior staff—should submit on an annual basis or in the event that they learn of a potential conflict of interest. Once the conflict of interest is documented, then the individual should be excused from the conversation/vote whenever such participation would be inappropriate. The minutes should reflect that Ms. or Mr. X was excused from the discussion on the nonprofit's insurance coverage because he or she is a member of the insurance company's board. Again, the size of the board is not important. What is important is that everyone on the board and on the senior management team discloses any real or potential conflicts of interest and does not take part in discussions or decisions related to the conflict of interest.

- *Secure adequate insurance.* The nonprofit and the board need to be adequately protected. It is essential that the nonprofit purchase directors and officers liability, general liability, business interruption, automobile, property and casualty, and other important insurance coverage. The nonprofit's insurance professional is a key player on this team. He or she can provide advice on the types of policies that are right for your organization.

- *Keep informed about current regulatory practices.* The proceedings of the Grassley hearings, the report of the Independent Sector's Panel on the Nonprofit Sector, and agencies such as the IRS provide materials for people to keep abreast of current developments in the legislative environment.

- *Review the suggestions in this book,* and consider how each best practice would "look" in your nonprofit. Some of the best practices are not size-sensitive. For example, a conflict of interest policy and a code of ethics are necessary in nonprofits of all sizes. Have your nonprofit's legal counsel assist you with the language. If your nonprofit does not currently have legal counsel, now is the time to obtain assistance. If your nonprofit requires pro bono assistance, contact your state or local bar association. Attorneys are expected to do a certain amount of pro bono work. You might also want to contact your local or regional nonprofit clearinghouse for assistance.

Summary

Your small nonprofit can have an excellent board and an excellent infrastructure and be in compliance with SOX. The size of the organization does not matter. What does matter is the commitment of the board and senior management to the nonprofit's mission and vision. The implementation of SOX requirements and best practices will serve to strengthen your small nonprofit so that it can withstand organizational growing pains and weather any circumstances that might confront its service to the community.

Letter from Senator Grassley to the Acting Chair of the American University Board of Trustees

United States Senate

COMMITTEE ON FINANCE

WASHINGTON, DC 20510–6200

October 27, 2005

Thomas Gottschalk, Acting Chair of the Board
Office of the President
American University
4400 Massachusetts Ave., NW
Washington, D.C.

Dear Mr. Gottschalk:

I am deeply troubled by reports about the recent actions of the American University's ("AU") board of trustees in regards to payments to former president Mr. Benjamin Ladner related to Mr. Ladner's departure. The Finance Committee has been engaged in a bipartisan review of charities and reform of charities and it appears the AU board could be a poster child for why review and reform are necessary.

The Internal Revenue Code ("IRC") provides charities very special treatment. Most important is the exemption from income tax and the ability to receive tax-deductible contributions. It is therefore particularly troubling when an organization receives preferential tax treatment and then believes that it is proper to provide approximately $3.75 million in payments to an individual who has reportedly failed to pay taxes on nearly $400,000 in income (for the last three years) after the board terminated his employment. Such actions raise significant questions about what other things a charity that has such a cavalier attitude toward the tax laws might be doing, especially in light of escalating tuition increases.

To assist the committee its review of AU and the AU board's actions, the Committee requests the following.

1) IRC Section 4958 - Excess Benefit Transactions
    a. Provide copies of Mr. Ladner's employment contract, deferred compensation and severance plans and any other compensation arrangements, including expense reimbursements.

    b. Provide all material, discussion, legal opinions, compensation studies and analysis or other related items used by the AU board, compensation committee or other relevant governing body when making its decisions regarding Mr. Ladner's employment contract, deferred compensation and severance plans and any other compensation arrangements, including expense

1

reimbursements. Provide all material documenting AU's compliance with Internal Revenue Code (IRC) section 4958 with respect to these items, including but not limited to copies of minutes of meetings from AU's board, compensation committee or other relevant governing body as well resolutions or written actions regarding such transactions. Provide a copy of any settlement agreement or release of claims entered into with Mr. Ladner and explain how any amounts paid under such agreement were determined.

c. Identify consultants, accountants, lawyers and or other outside advisors used with respect to the items requested in "a" and "b" above, and include names, addresses and total fees paid.

d. Provide a list and brief description of all no-bid contracts issued by AU and its affiliates and subsidiaries over $100,000 for last 11 years. Explain how no-bid contracts are awarded.

e. Provide copies of any conflicts of interest or similar policies as well as expense reimbursement and travel policies that have been adopted. Include an explanation of how the AU processes expenses and requests for reimbursement. Please explain what, if any, changes to these policies AU is considering.   Explain whether such policies were followed and enforced with respect to Mr. Ladner

f. How did the board comply with its State law fiduciary duties in its actions regarding the hiring, retention, compensation of, and termination of, Mr. Ladner?

2) Board Governance & Transparency

a.. Discuss whether you believe that there is sufficient transparency regarding your highly compensated officers, directors, trustees and employees. What do you to ensure numbers are transparent historically and in the future. Do you believe there was adequate disclosure?

b. Provide descriptions of all transactions with disqualified persons (as defined in IRC section 4958(f)). Provide copies of legal opinions and minutes from board meetings discussing these transactions. Please provide this for the last three years for compensation, loans, property purchases/leases and services for over $100,000.

c. I understand that the AU audit of Mr. Ladner was for the most recent three years. However, Mr. Ladner's tenure was for eleven years. Given the extraordinarily troubling findings from the audit of the most recent time period, please inform me of your plans to conduct a complete audit of the entire 11 years.

d. Provide your articles of incorporation, bylaws (in effect for past 11 years), application for exempt status, and the IRS determination letter. For the past 11 years, please provide a brief description of individuals who served on the boards, a short biography, qualifications, how the

2

board member was selected and how the board members serve the interests of the community.

3) Internal Revenue Service Filings

a. Please inform me of whether AU plans to amend its Form 990 for any year and whether it will be necessary for AU to amend Forms 990-T or 1120 of any affiliated or subsidiary organizations.

b. Provide copies of all Forms 990-T and 1120 of affiliates and subsidiaries of AU for the last three years. Please provide all copies of legal opinions provided, created or received by AU for the past three years that discuss unrelated business income tax ("UBIT") implications, including debt-finance income as well as Real Estate Investment Trusts (REIT).

c. Disclose the identity of all supporting organizations (as defined in IRC section 509(a)(3)) and provide copies of Forms 990s for such organizations for the most recent three years.

d. Provide all correspondence with the IRS for the past five years.

e. AU's 2003 Form 990 indicates $180 million in tax-exempt bond liabilities. Please explain in detail what the proceeds were used for, and how soon after receipt bond proceeds were obligated.

f. Provide a copy of all work papers from KPMG audits for the last three years.

4) Executive Compensation

For the past three years for individuals listed in Part V of Form 990 "List of Officers, Directors, Trustees and Key Employees," and Part I "Compensation of the Five Highest Paid employees Other Than Officers, Directors and Trustees", please answer the following:

a. Explain how you established the amount of compensation and benefits.

b. Describe the nature of the components for each amount reported under compensation; contributions to employee benefit plans & deferred compensation; and, expense account and other allowances.

c. Describe the duties and responsibilities that each individual performed for you.

d. Do the amounts reported represent the total economic benefits each individual received from you for the year? If no, please explain what other benefits were received, including the fair market value of those benefits.

3

e. Did you establish the rebuttable presumption under section 53.4958-6 of the Foundation and Similar Excise Taxes Treasury Regulations as to the compensation and benefits reported for any of the individuals? If yes, please provide copies of all supporting documentation.

f. If the answer is no to "e" for any of the individuals, do you have documentation supporting the reasonableness of the compensation and benefits reported? If yes, please provide a copy of this documentation.

g. Did the AU board approve the amount of compensation and benefits reported? If yes, please provide a copy of the approval for each individual.

h. Did you have an employment contract or any other compensatory agreement with any of the individuals? If yes, please provide a copy of the contract or agreement.

i. Does the amount of compensation and benefits reported agree with the amount reported on each individual's Form W-2 or Form 1099? If no, please explain the difference.

j. Did any of these individuals use any property that you owned or leased (such as an automobile, aircraft, real estate, credit card, etc.) for any purpose other than to further the organization's exempt purposes? If yes, did you include the value of this usage in the amount of compensation and benefits reported? Was the value included on the individual's Form W-2 or Form 1099? If your answer to either of these questions is "No" please explain.

Thank you for your time and assistance. Please provide the answers to these questions by December 1, 2005. If you have any questions, please contact Mr. Dean Zerbe of my staff at (202) 224-4515.

Cordially yours,

Charles E. Grassley
Chairman

cc: Senator Baucus

4

Whistleblower Protection Policy

[Agency name
Street address
City, State, Zip code]

Whistleblower Protection Policy

The whistleblower protection policy is being implemented at the [agency name] to comply with the Public Company Accounting Reform and Investor Protection Act of 2002 (Sarbanes-Oxley). This provision in the legislation applies to all organizations, not just publicly traded ones.

At the [agency name], any staff member or volunteer who reports waste, fraud, or abuse will not be fired or otherwise retaliated against for making the report.

The report will be investigated and even if determined not to be waste, fraud, or abuse, the individual making the report will not be retaliated against. There will be no punishment for reporting problems—including firing, demotion, suspension, harassment, failure to consider the employee for promotion, or any other kind of discrimination.

There are several ways to make a report of suspected waste, fraud, or abuse:

- Call the anonymous hotline at [phone number].
- Send an e-mail to [e-mail address].
- Submit a report in writing.

Here is what we will do to investigate the report:

[The agency would list the steps it would take to investigate the allegation.]

Here is how we will follow up to report on our findings:

- Provide the person filing a report with a summary of our findings.
- Take steps to deal with the issue addressed, including making operational or personnel changes.
- If warranted, contact law enforcement to deal with any criminal activities.

Risk Management Plan and Business Continuity Plan

RISK MANAGEMENT PLAN: TABLE OF CONTENTS

Risk assessment report for the FY or calendar year 20XX

Nonprofit's profile—this section of the plan provides information on the nonprofit's current status. This section would describe the SOX best practices that the nonprofit has implemented.

Plan of action to address the risk assessment report

First-priority risks—these risks are the ones that the nonprofit will address first. For each risk, describe:

- Resources needed to address the risk
- Techniques for each risk
- Responsibilities and timelines
- Desired outcomes/measurements of success
- Documentation of prior claims, occurrences

Second-priority risks—these are the risks that the nonprofit will address after the primary risks have been treated. These could also be the primary risks for the next round of risk assessment:

- Resources needed to address these risks
- Techniques for each risk

- Responsibilities and timelines
- Desired outcomes/measurements of success
- Documentation of prior claims, occurrences

Other sections of risk management plan:

- Important documents—insurance policies (declaration sheet only). Include just the cover page of each of your insurance policies (i.e., the page that has the limits of the coverage listed on it).
- Phone numbers of insurance professional, attorney, board of directors, other key staff, and volunteers.

Risks to be considered for next FY or calendar year—this is the section of the plan in which emerging issues can be documented.

Business Continuity Plan

This sample plan provides a fill-in-the-blanks method of developing an initial business continuity plan. Once the initial plan is compiled, your nonprofit will be able to see how the plan can customized to meet your organization's needs. It is very important to include only the information that is necessary and sufficient. There should be systems in place to back up files, databases, and other critical information so that your nonprofit can resume operations in another location if necessary.

Emergency Protocols

This section of the plan should:

- Include a floorplan(s) for each floor in your nonprofit—he emergency exits should be shown clearly.
- Include information on fire alarms (if applicable) and smoke detectors and instructions for evacuating the building in the event of an emergency.
- Provide instructions for dealing with the type of emergencies that are appropriate to your geographic location (i.e., earthquakes, tornadoes, etc.).
- Give the location of fire extinguishers, first aid kits, and flashlights.

- Ensure that fire extinguishers are current and are inspected and recharged as appropriate.
- Identify those individuals who are first aid and CPR certified.

Contact Information for Board Members and Staff

Important! The data contained in this worksheet is confidential material and should have very limited distribution.

You can paste the contact information for all board, staff members, and key volunteers in this section of the plan. The following categories of information should be provided for everyone on the list:

Name

Address

Home phone

Office phone

Cell phone

Family member's cell phone number

Pager

Fax

Business e-mail address

Personal e-mail address

Business Resumption Strategies for Each Department within Your Nonprofit

Complete a strategy sheet like this one for every department within your nonprofit.

- For each department or function within your nonprofit, list the most important activities or tasks that have to be done to remain in operation.
- List the ways in which the nonprofit can ensure that these functions can continue or resume—perhaps at another location.
- List the materials and/or supplies that would be needed to resume these functions if the nonprofit's offices are completely destroyed.

- Provide an inventory of furnishings, equipment, and specialized software/hardware and other technology needs.

- Cross train the staff. It is essential to ensure that more than one individual knows how to do each important task or function.

Communication

- *Internal communication.* Identify the strategy for communicating with the board, staff, volunteers, and clients about the nature of the business interruption and how to contact the nonprofit.

- *External communication.* Prepare a general statement that can be retrieved in the event of a business interruption. The statement should identify the name of the nonprofit, the name of the spokesperson, and contact information for the spokesperson; and provide a general description of what happened (the fewer the details the better) and information about the location of the nonprofit and how to make an emergency donation (if applicable).

- List contact information for the local media.

Financial Services

[Confidential—include this section only in the copies of the plan distributed to the executive committee of the board, the executive officer, and the chief financial officer.]

In this section of the plan, include the account information for all financial accounts—banks, investments, and other financial instruments. The purpose of this section is to have the information available on a need-to-know basis for those senior board and staff members who are authorized to make transactions with your nonprofit's bank and other financial service providers. For each bank and/or financial service provider, provide this information:

- Signature authority for your nonprofit—list the names and contact information for all signatories

- Bank codes and other security access information

Vendors

Vendors are very important people to your nonprofit in the event of a serious business interruption. As you determine which vendors to include, consider commercial real estate agents, plumbers, electricians, locksmiths, window-repair, and the like. Information technology vendors are always important, particularly if your nonprofit has to relocate.

Have at least the following information available for each vendor:

Vendor name

Contact person for your nonprofit's account with the vendor

Customer service manager (if the contact person is not available)

Phone number

Cell phone or pager

Fax number

Your nonprofit's account number

Person at your nonprofit who is authorized to place an order

Alternate person

Address of vendor

Service Providers—Utilities, Water, Governmental Agencies

Have at least the following information available for each vendor:

Contact person at the agency

Phone number

Cell phone or pager

Fax number

Your nonprofit's identifying information (account number or ID number)

Person at your nonprofit who is authorized to interact with the agency

Alternate person

Address of agency

If Your Nonprofit Needs to Relocate

In this section, outline the materials and data that would be needed to resume operations in an alternative location. As you determine what you will need, also consider the sources of these materials and the account numbers and/or security codes that will be necessary to access the materials and data.

- Vendors
- Essential equipment and material to support the critical functions of this department
- Contacts, account numbers, and security codes—identify the individuals who are in possession of this data
- Other materials needed

Technology Policy

TALKING POINTS

Key areas for explanation in a technology policy include:

- All aspects of the nonprofit's technology belongs to the nonprofit. There are no expectations of personal privacy when using the nonprofit's technology.
- E-mail and web access belong to the nonprofit.
- Examples of inappropriate e-mail messages:
  - Jokes
  - Harassment
  - Political commentary, particularly hate messages
  - Anything you would not want to read on the front page of your local newspaper or have CNN broadcast
- The policy covers all of the nonprofit's technology: hardware and software, including laptop computers, desktop computers, hand-held devices such as PDAs and BlackBerries, cell phones, Internet access, e-mail, and all software programs purchased through the nonprofit.
- All electronic devices, such as laptops and PDAs, must be returned when a person leaves the employ or volunteer assignment of the nonprofit.
- Specify the policy on the storage and transportation of sensitive information on laptops that leave your premises.

- Managers, staff, and volunteers who are entrusted with the nonprofit's cell phones, laptops, PDAs, or other electronics need to understand that they will be held personally accountable for the safety of the equipment, the safe use of the equipment, and the security of the data stored on these devices.

Review of Internal Controls Report and Recommendations

OVERVIEW OF THE PROJECT

Describe:

- Scope of the review and why it is being conducted
- What the process for the review entails
- Expected deliverables from the review

SYSTEMS

Explain why the emphasis is on internal systems, and express (chart out if necessary) the types of interdependencies that exist within the agency's internal systems. For every department, provide a brief description of each of its systems and discuss what other departments depend on that department. For example:

- *Finance.* Describe the systems of internal controls, the systems for payroll, receivables, and payables.
- *Information management.* Describe the systems within the broad range of technology, such as e-mail, intranet, Internet access, software interdependency, and mobile technology, including cell phones, PDAs, and laptops.

- *Human resources.* Describe the required policies that are (or will be put) in place, such as whistleblower protection, and how staff files are developed and kept up to date. Describe how performance expectations and performance reviews are coordinated. Describe other processes, such as worker compensation claims process, benefit package administration, sick leave, and vacation time administration.

- *Operations.* Describe the systems related to document retention (or identify if this system needs to be introduced), client intake and service, programmatic design and delivery, development, and other aspects of the agency's operations.

- *Governance.* Describe the agency's governance system in terms of process for agenda development, strategic decision making, board recruitment, and staffing.

- *Other areas of the nonprofit.* Describe systems unique to the agency.

RECOMMENDATIONS AND TIMELINE

This section presents recommendations for those systems and policies that are specified by recent legislation (SOX or equivalent state law) and those systems and policies that need to be introduced to establish greater transparency and efficiency. Establish a reasonable timeline and assign specific staff members to complete the deliverables identified in this section. For each deliverable, assign a staff member who will be accountable for the deliverable. Decide what you would be able to accomplish in:

- One month
- Three months
- Six months

Set a deadline for completing all of the systems/proof by 10 months from the start of the project. Book a look-back date (at the end of 10 months) to determine if further work is needed.

Board of Directors— Governance Profile and Performance Expectations

This document outlines the roles and duties of the board, including the distinction between governance roles and management roles within the nonprofit.

OVERSIGHT AND POLICY MAKING

- Supervise executive director (ED) or CEO of the nonprofit
- Oversight in areas of:
  - Financial operations
  - Internal controls
  - Compliance with federal, state, and local laws and regulations
  - Ultimate control and authority and responsibility for the nonprofit operations

TERM LIMITS

All board members should be subject to term limits. When a board member joins the board, it should be for a specified number of years. There should also be a specified number of consecutive terms that a board member can hold (usually two). There is no point in having term limits if a member can serve indefinitely. There should also be a specified number of years that the person must be off of the board before he or she can be allowed to rejoin the board. Former board members can certainly be assigned to other projects or committees, such as the audit committee, to take advantage of their knowledge and skills.

SUMMARY OF BOARD COMMITTEES' DESCRIPTIONS AND PERFORMANCE OBJECTIVES

Here are some types of committees that could be useful to your nonprofit. Not all nonprofits need every committee, so choose what works for you.

- Finance committee
- Audit committee
- Development and fundraising committee
- Personnel committee
- Nominating committee (for the board of directors)
- Facilities committee
- Strategic planning committee
- Risk management committee

PROCESS FOR BOARD MEMBER NOMINATION AND ELECTION

Here is a recommended process for identifying suitable board candidates, screening the candidates, and preparing a slate for board consideration.

1. Develop a list of potential candidates for the board through board member suggestions, networking, and by means of a community nonprofit clearinghouse.

2. Speak informally with each potential candidate to determine his or her interest in joining the board, the candidate's individual credentials, and suitability.

3. Allow those candidates who express interest to observe one or two of the nonprofit's board meetings.

4. The nominating committee arranges for formal interviews with those candidates who would like to be considered. Discuss board member obligations and performance expectations with candidates. Ask candidates to present either a recent résumé or curriculum vitae.

5. The nominating committee presents the slate of candidates to the board. The board has been given the candidates' résumés/CVs prior to the board meeting. A vote is taken on the slate, or by individual candidate.

6. Notify candidates by phone and a follow-up formal letter congratulating them on their election to the board. Also tell new board members when the board orientation will take place (see the next section for an orientation lesson plan) and how they can expect to receive a binder with board materials. In addition, provide new board members with a conflict of interest letter for their completion and signature. Pair each new board member with a current board member as a mentor.

Board Orientation Session

The session should be approximately 60 to 90 minutes in length. The learning objectives of this orientation include:

- New board members understand the nonprofit's mission, vision, and strategic plan.
- New board members have an understanding of the nonprofit's history so that they can appreciate where the organization has been and where it is headed.
- New board members understand their obligations and performance objectives.
- New board members understand board policies on meetings, attendance, conflict of interest, and other policies that emerge from SOX best practices.
- New board members have received their job descriptions and understand their performance expectations and fiduciary obligations as board members.

Outline of Curriculum

- Introductions
- *Agency's mission, vision, and strategic plan.* This segment of the orientation provides an overview of the nonprofit's mission, vision, and strategic plan. These documents should be part of the new board member's "board binder."
- *Agency's history.* This segment of the orientation should provide new board members with a brief history of the organization. Use of a timeline to describe important events in the organization's history can be helpful.
- *Being a board member.* This section reviews the expectations of all board members. Particular emphasis should be on describing board member legal duties of care, loyalty, and obedience. Explain why board members are required to sign an annual conflict of interest letter and why they need to review materials carefully before board meetings. It is important that the discussion parallels the materials found in the "board binder," but also allow time for questions and answers.
- *Board member performance expectations.* This segment reviews the material in the "board binder" on attendance requirements, conflict of interest policy, fiduciary obligations, financial support of the agency, code of ethics, and keeping informed about the agency's operations.
- *Board member job description.* This section is really a summary of the previous two sections and is presented so that board members understand their role in a more integrated fashion. If the agency has a committee system, describe how board members are placed on committees and performance expectations for committee members.
- *Role of the board mentor.* If the new board member has been paired up with a seasoned board member, describe how the interaction will serve to enrich the new board member's experience and provide him or her with a resource for questions or learning.

Board Binder Contents

- Agency mission and vision statements
- Agency strategic plan

- Brief history of the agency
- Financial statements from the past three months
- Development and fundraising profile of the agency
- Board member legal duties: care, loyalty, obedience
- Board policies:
  - Meeting attendance and preparation expectations
  - Fiduciary obligations and conflict of interest policies
  - Financial support of the agency
  - Code of ethics
- Committee structure [if applicable]
- Board roster
- Staff roster

Conflict-of-Interest Policy

A conflict-of-interest policy and set of procedures, including a disclosure statement, need to be in place for the purposes of educating the board on its legal obligation of loyalty and on what constitutes a conflict of interest. Procedures need to be in place to disclose real and potential conflicts of interest and deal with these disclosed conflicts appropriately in subsequent board discussion and voting. All board and senior management need to complete a conflict-of-interest statement on an annual basis. Board minutes need to reflect a member's abstention from discussion and voting on a topic that presents a conflict of interest.

Talking Points

Here are some reasons why real or potential conflicts of interest need to be disclosed:

- The legal standard of loyalty requires board members to put the financial interests of the nonprofit ahead of any personal gain. One way to achieve this is to identify those relationships and/or business dealings that either present a conflict of interest or have the potential for being a conflict of interest.

- By signing a letter indicating real or potential conflicts of interest, or stating that the individual has none, the nonprofit has a record of those areas that may pose a conflict of interest for individual board members. The nonprofit can then take steps to ensure that the individual board member does not take part in discussions or votes related to those areas.

- Transparency and full disclosure are very important in today's nonprofit environment.

Procedures for Dealing with Conflict of Interest

- Conflict-of-interest letters are signed on an annual basis.
- When a board discussion addresses an area that has been identified as a conflict of interest, the individual involved is excused from the discussion and not permitted to vote. This is recorded in the minutes of the meeting.
- The board reserves the right to ask an individual who presents a very serious conflict of interest to resign from the board or be placed in a capacity that neutralizes a conflict of interest.

SAMPLE CONFLICT-OF-INTEREST LETTER

[Agency name
Street address
City, State, Zip code]

[Date
[Board member name
Street address
City, State, Zip code]

Please complete and sign this annual conflict-of-interest statement. We appreciate your hard work on the [agency name] Board.

I, [board member name], state that I have/do not have the following personal, business, or professional relationships that may present a conflict of interest:

(Circle appropriate statement.)

I do not have any conflicts of interest.

I have the following relationships or business interests that may pose a conflict of interest:

(List those relationships and businesses that might pose as conflict of interest.)

As a member of the [agency name] Board, I commit to placing the agency's interest and gain ahead of my own, and will further commit to excusing myself from any discussion or votes related to those areas in which I may have a conflict of interest.

Signed,

[Board member name

Date]

Code of Ethics for Board and Senior Management

This policy describes the types of behavioral expectations that relate to the roles of board member and member of senior management and establishes a confidential means by which employees or volunteers can raise ethical concerns. One particularly significant provision is the prohibition against any type of loan or financial gift by the nonprofit to a board member or member of the staff at any level. Note: Board, staff, and volunteers should be required to read/sign the code of ethics.

Ensure that each category addresses how the nonprofit commits to being in compliance with laws and regulations, being accountable to the public, and responsibly handling resources.

TALKING POINTS

- Organizational values that are present or expressed in the nonprofit's mission and other supporting documents such as strategic plans
- Mission
- Governance
- Conflicts of interest
- Legal compliance
- Responsible stewardship of resources and financial oversight
- Openness and disclosure

- Professional integrity, as ethical behavior would relate to all aspects of services rendered and in the process of development/fundraising
- Other issues that relate to how your nonprofit operates

SAMPLE CODE OF ETHICS FOR A NONPROFIT BOARD MEMBER

[Agency name
Street address
City, State, Zip code]

Board Member Code of Ethics

As a member of the [agency name] Board, I will:

- Endeavor at all times to place the interest of the [agency name] above my own.
- Be diligent in the performance of my duties, come prepared to all board meetings, and fulfill my obligations as a board member.
- Not seek or accept any personal financial gain from my membership on the board of the [agency name].
- Seek to continually improve my knowledge of the [agency name] and the nonprofit sector.
- Strive to establish and maintain dignified and honorable relationships with my fellow board members, the [agency name] staff, clients, and donors.
- Strive to improve the public understanding of the mission and vision of the [agency name].
- Obey all laws and regulations and avoid any conduct or activity that would cause harm to the [agency name].

Bibliography

ABA Coordinating Committee on Nonprofit Governance. *Guide to Nonprofit Corporate Governance in the Wake of Sarbanes-Oxley. American Bar Association* 4, no. 6 (July 2005).

AICPA. Sarbanes-Oxley Act/PCAOB Implementation Central. www.aicpa.org/sarbanes/index.asp.

Association of Certified Fraud Examiners. *Report to the Nation, 1996,* from www.cfenet.com/pdfs/Report_to_the_Nation.pdf.

Babcock, Charles R., and Judith Havemann. "Managing an Agency and Image," *Washington Post,* February 16, 1999.

Barstow, David. "In Congress, Harsh Words for Red Cross," *New York Times,* November 7, 2001.

Better Business Bureau Wise Giving Alliance. *Standards for Charity Accountability.* Arlington, VA, Spring 2003.

Bingham McCutchen LLP. *Silicon Valley Update: Corporate Governance in Entrepreneurial and Large Corporation.* NACD Northern California Chapter. January 15, 2004.

BoardSource and Independent Sector. (2003). "The Sarbanes-Oxley Act and Implications for Nonprofit Organizations," from www.boardsource.org/clientfiles/Sarbanes-Oxley.pdf.

Bumgardner, L. J. "How Does the Sarbanes-Oxley Act Impact American Business?" *Journal of Contemporary Business Practice* 6, no. 1 (2003). From http://gbr.pepperdine.edu/031/sarbanesoxley.html.

COSO (1999). *Fraudulent Financial Reporting: 1987–1997. An Analysis of U.S. Public Companies. Executive Summary and Introduction.* www.coso.org/publications/executive_summary_fraudulent_financial_reporting.htm.

COSO (1992). *Internal Control—Integrated Framework: Executive Summary.* www.coso.org/publications/executive_summary_integrated_framework.htm.

DeLucia, Michael S. "Practical Guide to Major Changes Now Under Discussion in the Nonprofit Sector," *New Hampshire Bar Journal* (Spring 2005).

Dickens, Charles. *A Christmas Carol.* New York: Bantam Classic, 1986.

Dodd, Jill S. "New Bill Would Affect the Governance of Nonprofits." FindLaw, http://library.findlaw.com/2004/Oct/28/133625.html.

Evans, Will. "State to Turn a Critical Eye on Its Charities: Governor Signs Law That Requires Tighter Auditing Procedures," *Sacramento Bee,* October 3, 2004.

Evergreen State Society (2003). "What Is Form 990?: How Is It Used?" www.nonprofits.org/npofaq/19/06.html.

Everson, Mark W., Commissioner of the Internal Revenue Service. Testimony before the U.S. Senate Finance Committee hearings on "Charity Oversight and Reform: Keeping Bad Things from Happening to Good Charities," Washington, DC, June 2004.

Everson, Mark W., Commissioner of the Internal Revenue Service. Testimony before the U.S. Senate Finance Committee hearings on "Charities and Charitable Giving: Proposals for Reform," Washington, DC, April 2005.

Falvey, Jack. "Socratic Guidance for the Boardroom," *Wall Street Journal,* December 7, 2005.

Feder, Barnaby J. "Peter F. Drucker, A Pioneer in Social and Management Theory, Is Dead at 95," *New York Times,* November 12, 2005.

Felch, Jason, and Robin Fields. "Senator Rebukes Getty: Finance Panel Chair Says the Trust Hasn't Curbed CEO Barry Munitz's Lavish Expenses," *Los Angeles Times,* June 23, 2005.

Gallegher, Brian. Testimony before the U.S. Senate Finance Committee hearings on "Charities and Charitable Giving: Proposals for Reform," Washington, DC, April 2005.

Gill, Mel. *Practical Lessons from Case Studies on 20 Canadian Nonprofits.* Institute on Governance, Ottawa, Canada, 2001.

Guidestar. "How Nonprofits Have Responded to Sarbanes-Oxley: August Question of the Month Results." www.Guidestar.org/news/features/question_aug05.

Grassley, Charles. Letter to Marsha Evans, Washington DC, August 12, 2002.

Grassley, Charles. Letter to Thomas Gottschalk, Acting Chair of the Board, American University, Washington, DC, October 27, 2005.

Greenberg, Daniel S. "Blood, Politics, and the American Red Cross," *The Lancet* 358 (November 2001).

Hawkins, Sarah. "Nonprofits Face Regulatory Measures," Tech Soup. www.techsoup.org/print/printpage.cfm?newsid=1717&type=news.

Healy, Bernadine, M.D. Letter to Kathryn Forbes and Norman Augustine, Washington DC, April 3, 2001.

Healy, Bernadine M.D., *Memorandum to Ron Lund*, Washington, DC, April 16, 2001.

Herman, M. L., G. L. Head, and P. M. Jackson. *Managing Risk in Nonprofit Organizations: A Comprehensive Guide* (Hoboken, NJ: John Wiley & Sons, 2004).

Holmes, Sarah A., Margaret Langford, O. James Welch, and Sandra T. Welch. "Associations Between Internal Controls and Organizational Citizenship Behavior," *Journal of Managerial Issues* 14, no. 1 (Spring 2002).

Hopkins, Bruce. "Sarbanes-Oxley Act of 2002: What It Means for Nonprofit Organizations," *Nonprofit Counsel* 19, no. 10 (October 2002).

Independent Sector. "Learning from Sarbanes-Oxley: A Checklist for Nonprofits and Foundations." Washington, DC, 2004.

Independent Sector, Panel on the Nonprofit Sector. *Report to Congress and the Nonprofit Sector on Governance, Transparency and Accountability*. Washington, DC, June 2005.

Internal Revenue Service. "Corporate Responsibility," Ann. 2002-87, 37.

Internal Revenue Service. Publication 463, "Travel, Entertainment, Gift and Car Expenses," 2004.

Internal Revenue Service. "Internal Revenue Bulletin." IR Bulletin 1999-17, from www.irs.gov/pub/irs-irbs/irb99-17.pdf.

Internal Revenue Service. "Political Lobbying and Political Activities," from www.irs.gov/charities/charitable/article/0,,id=120703,00.html.

Jackson, Peggy M., and Toni E. Fogarty. *Sarbanes-Oxley for Nonprofits* (Hoboken, NJ: John Wiley & Sons, 2005).

Jackson, Peggy M., and Toni E. Fogarty. *Sarbanes-Oxley for Nonprofit Management* (Hoboken, NJ: John Wiley & Sons, 2006).

Jacobs, Jerald. "Conflict of Interest Policies—Address Them Now," *Association Management* 55 (May 2003).

Johnson, Carrie. "Charities Going Beyond Required Controls to Regain Their Donors' Confidence," *Washington Post*, April 6, 2005.

Johnson, Chip. "Watching the Police's Watchdogs," *San Francisco Chronicle*, August 13, 2004.

Jones, J. "Panel on the Nonprofit Sector Issues Report," *The NonProfit Times*. www.nptimes.com/Apr05/npt1.html.

Jones, Jeff. "Special Report: The Year in Review," *The Nonprofit Times* (December 2004).

Kosinski, Gregory, and Jay M. Cohen. "Fundamentals of Compliance," IDA/Kahn conference proceedings, San Jose, CA, May 2004.

Kuhn, N. O. "Intermediate Sanctions on NPO Executives," *Journal of Accountancy* (2001). www.aicpa.org/pubs/jofa/nov2001/kuhn.htm.

Lambert, Joyce. "Reduce Your Losses from Errors and Fraud," *Nonprofit World* 16, no. 5 (September/October 1998): 46–49.

Lange, Michele. "Keeping Your Head: New Sarbanes-Oxley Rules Make Document Retention Dizzying," *Corporate Counsel Magazine* (April 2003).

Larsen, K. "Summary: SB1262 'The Nonprofit Integrity Act,'" *California Association of Nonprofits* (2004). www2.niac.org/Documents/DocumentRetrieve .cfm?q_DocumentID=147&UploadDocClass=DynamicContent.

Levine, Samantha. "Red Crossroads: The Nation's Best-Known Charity Is Under Fire for How It Spends September 11th Disaster Funds," *U.S. News & World Report*, November 19, 2001.

Light, Paul C. Fact Sheet on the Continued Crisis in Charitable Confidence. Brookings Institution, Washington, DC, September 13, 2004.

Lindbloom, E. E. "The Sciences of 'Muddling Through.'" In *Readings in Modern Organizations*, edited by A. Etzioni, 154–165 (Englewood Cliffs, NJ: Prentice-Hall, 1969).

Longest, Beaufort B. Jr. "Eight Questions Every Board Needs to Answer," *Nonprofit World* 22, no. 3 (May/June 2004).

Markon, Jerry. "Ex-Chief of Local United Way Sentenced," *Washington Post*, May 15, 2004.

Maryland Association of Nonprofit Organizations. "Standards for Excellence: An Ethics and Accountability Code for the Nonprofit Sector." Baltimore, MD, 2004.

McDonough, Siobhan. "Survey: Charity CEO Raises Nearly Double Inflation Rate," *Advocate* (Baton Rouge, LA), September 27, 2004.

McLennan, Douglas. "Culture Clash: Has the Business Model for Arts Institutions Outlived Its Usefulness?" *Wall Street Journal*, October 8, 2005.

Mondaq Business Briefing. "Governance and Nonprofit Corporations: Requirements and Expectations in a Post–Sarbanes-Oxley World," May 20, 2004.

Mondaq Business Briefing. "Nonprofit Governance Reforms: Five Steps Toward Improved Accountability," May 25, 2004.

Moskin, Julia. "Thousands Missing in Revenue Records of Culinary Charity," *New York Times*, September 6, 2004.

National Association of Veterans' Research and Education Foundations. "Impact of the 2002 Sarbanes-Oxley Act (SOX) on Nonprofits," Washington, DC, 2005.

Nonprofit Integrity Act. State of California, State Senate Bill 1262, September 2004.

Nonprofit Leadership and Administration Faculty, Western Michigan University. "Nonprofit Management Governance Checkup," Fall 1999.

Office of the Attorney General, State of California. "Attorney General Lockyer Unveils Reforms to Toughen Nonprofit Accountability, Fundraiser Controls," February 12, 2004.

Office of the Attorney General, State of California. "FAQ on Nonprofit Integrity Act of 2004," January 2005.

Office of the Attorney General, State of California. "Summary of Key Provisions of the Nonprofit Integrity Act of 2004," October 2004.

O'Reilly-Allen, Margaret. "How to Have an Audit Without Breaking the Bank," *Nonprofit World* 20, no. 4 (July/August 2002).

Owens, John R. III. "Nonprofits Without Audit Committees Risk Disaster," *Nonprofit World* 22, no. 2 (March/April 2004).

Owens, Marcus S. "Sarbanes-Oxley: What It Means to Nonprofits." Caplin & Drysdale, Chartered, Washington, DC, 2004.

Panel on the Nonprofit Sector. "Final Report of the Panel," *Independent Sector* (2005). www.nonprofitpanel.org/final/.

Panetta, Leon. Testimony before the U.S. Senate Finance Committee hearings on "Charities and Charitable Giving: Proposals for Reform," Washington, DC, April 2005.

Peregrine, Michael W., and James R. Schwartz. "Taking the Prudent path: Best Practices for Not-for-Profit Boards," *Trustee* (Chicago, IL) 56, no. 10 (November/December 2003).

Perkins, John. "Sensemaking: A Remedy for Indecisive Boards," *Nonprofit World* (January/February 2001).

PricewaterhouseCoopers LLP. United Way of the National Capital Area Forensic Accounting Investigation, Washington, DC, August 7, 2003.

Reaves, Cynthia F. "The Impact of the Sarbanes-Oxley Act of 2002 on Nonprofit Ethics," *Michigan Business Law Journal* (Summer 2003).

Revised Model Nonprofit Corporation Act (1987). *http://www.muridae.com/nporegulation/documents/model_npo_corp_act.html*

San Francisco Chronicle, Daily Digest, "Former WorldCom Directors to Pay $18 million in Cash," January 6, 2005.

Savstrom, Curtis. "Expanding Sarbanes-Oxley to Nonprofit Organizations," Health Care Compliance Association (June 2004).

Schein, Edgar. *Organizational Culture and Leadership*, 2nd ed. (San Francisco: Jossey-Bass, 1992).

Schroeder, Mike. "Is It Time to Rethink Your Board's Structure?" *Nonprofit World* 21, no. 6 (November/December 2003).

Schweitzer, Carole. "The Board Balancing Act: Achieving Board Accountability Without Micromanaging," *Association Management* 56, no. 1 (January 2004).

Schwinn, Elizabeth, and Grant Williams. "IRS Outlines Audit Plans for Nonprofit Organizations," *Chronicle of Philanthropy*, October 16, 2003.

Silk, Thomas. "Corporate Scandals and the Governance of Nonprofit Organizations," *Exempt Organization Tax Review* 38, no. 3 (December 2002).

Silk, Thomas. "Ten Emerging Principles of Governance of Nonprofit Corporations," *Exempt Organization Tax Review* 43, no. 1 (January 2004).

Silverman, Rachel Emma. "Charities to Start to Grade Themselves," *Wall Street Journal*, August 18, 2004.

Sinclair, Matthew. "Nonprofit Whistleblowers Need Protection," *Nonprofit Times*, June 1, 2004.

Snyder, Gary. "Boards Must Change the Way They Do Business," *Nonprofit World* 21, no. 4 (July/August 2003).

Sontag, Deborah. "Who Brought Bernadine Healy Down?" *New York Times Magazine*, December 23, 2001.

Stamer, C. M. "IRS Plans to Put Tax-Exempt Organizations Under Microscope," *Houston Business Journal* (2004). www.bizjournals.com/houston/stories/2004/09/06/focus2.html.

Strom, Stephanie. "Questions About Some Charities' Activities Lead to a Push for Tighter Regulation," *New York Times*, March 21, 2004.

Strom, Stephanie. "Public Confidence in Charities Stays Flat," *New York Times*, September 13, 2004.

Stroot, S., et al. *Peer Assistance and Review Guidebook* (Columbus, OH: Ohio Department of Education, 1998).

Sun, Lena H. "Red Cross to Give All Funds to Victims," *Washington Post*, November 15, 2001.

Swards, P., V. Bjorklund, and J. Small. "How to Read the IRS Form 990 & Find Out What It Means," Nonprofit Coordinating Committee of New York (2003). www.npccny.org/Form_990/990.htm.

Taggart, Stephanie P. "Nonprofits to Face Sarbanes-Oxley–Like Reforms," *Northeast Pennsylvania Business Journal* via, 2005.

Taylor, Karla. "Changing Expectations for Nonprofit Governance," *Association Management* (January 2005).

Tyler, J. Larry, and Errol L. Biggs. "Conflict of Interest: Strategies for Remaining 'Purer Than Caesar's Wife,'" *Trustee* 57, no. 3 (March 2004).

United States Senate Finance Committee. Staff Discussion Paper ("Grassley White Paper") released in conjunction with June 2004 hearings on "Charity Oversight and Reform: Keeping Bad Things from Happening to Good Charities." Washington, DC, June 2004.

Vail, John P., and Joshua Mintz. "Governance of Not-for-Profit Organizations in 2003," Quarles and Brady LLP, Chicago, IL, June 6, 2003.

Vishneski, John S. III. "New Liabilities Created by Sarbanes-Oxley: Are Your Directors, Officers Covered?" *National Underwriter*, December 1, 2003.

Wallack, Todd. "Nonprofit Advisory Group in Crisis, Management Center Helped Local Agencies," *San Francisco Chronicle*, January 22, 2004.

Wallack, Todd. "Charity Settles in Pipevine Fiasco," *San Francisco Chronicle*, February 19, 2004.

Wallack, Todd. "SF Nonprofit to Shut Down," *San Francisco Chronicle*, May 19, 2004.

Wallack, Todd. "Nonprofits Fight Tougher Disclosure Rules," *San Francisco Chronicle*, June 24, 2004.

Walters, Brent R. "Nonprofits Are Corporations Too: Now It's Time for Iowa to Treat Them That Way," *Journal of Corporation Law* (Iowa City, IA) 28, no. 1 (Fall 2002).

Weidenfeld, Edward L. "Sarbanes-Oxley and Fiduciary Best Practices for Officers and Directors of Nonprofit Organizations," *Tax Management Estates, Gifts and Trusts Journal*, March 11, 2004.

Weiner, Stanley. "Proposed Legislation: Its Impact on Not-for-Profit Board Governance," *CPA Journal* 73, no. 11 (November 2003).

Werther, William B. Jr., Evan Berman, and Karen Echols. "The Three Roles of Nonprofit Management," *Nonprofit World* 23, no. 5 (September/October 2005).

Wolverton, Brad. "What Went Wrong? Board Actions at Issue at Troubled D.C. United Way," *Chronicle of Philanthropy*, September 4, 2003.

Disclaimer

Important! The language in these samples is not intended as legal advice, and the talking points are not legal recommendations. You need to consult with your legal advisor to ensure that the language and design of any of the documents that you prepare are appropriate to the needs of your nonprofit.

Index